ROUGH
GUIDES

POCKET **ROUGH GUIDE**
BERLIN

This sixth edition updated by
Matthew Pearson

T0343653

CONTENTS

BERLIN

Of all today's European capitals, Berlin carries the biggest buzz. In the three and a half decades since it was reunified, the city has developed into a heady meld of grit and glamour that's vastly different from anywhere else in Germany – or the rest of the world for that matter. Its edgy cultural and fashion scenes, unsurpassed nightlife and radical anti-gentrification agenda regularly make global headlines, as does its reputation as "poor but sexy" – a term coined by former mayor Klaus Wowereit and quickly adopted as the city's unofficial motto.

Statues in front of Berliner Dom

The crackle of youthful energy that characterizes much of the inner city – especially areas such as trendy Mitte (Spandauer Vorstadt and around), student-heavy Friedrichshain and artist and expat haven Neukölln – mingles incongruously with the scars of Berlin's harrowing past. Holocaust memorials, concentration camps and a wealth of thought-provoking museums, such as Daniel Libeskind's celebrated Jewish Museum, join bullet holes and empty spaces to provide visitors with constant reminders of the horrors of National Socialism and World War II. The fragments of the Berlin Wall, scattered around the city like broken concrete teeth, testify to its painful division – sometimes still reflected in the mindsets of the city's formerly divided neighbourhoods, many of which have retained their pre-reunification identities.

So overwhelming is Berlin's twentieth-century history and its twenty-first-century grab for the future, that it's easy to forget that the city has a longer and more illustrious history. Originally two cities – Cölln, an island in the middle of the city, now the site of the Museum Island, and Alt Berlin, formerly a fishing village – Berlin was formed in 1237. Located at the intersection of significant trade routes, it quickly prospered, rising to power as the seat of the Hohenzollern dynasty following the Thirty Years' War. During the eighteenth century, Frederick the Great (1712–86) established Berlin – and neighbouring Potsdam, with

Oberbaum Bridge

its magnificent summer palace Sanssouci – as a grand capital for the Prussian monarchy; it was during this time that many of the buildings on Unter den Linden were constructed. When Germany was united in 1871, Berlin became its capital.

Following the defeat of World War I, during the Weimar Republic (1919–33) the city rivalled Paris as a centre for the cultural avant-garde, the legacy and spirit of which live on in contemporary Berlin. World War II reduced seventy percent of the city to ruins, and it was partitioned into American, British and French zones in the West and a Soviet zone in the East. The three Western-occupied zones eventually merged

When to visit

Berlin is a great city to visit at any time of year with plenty to do and see – but like most places, it really comes alive in the warmer months. If you're not a fan of cold weather, be warned that the winter months can be brutally chilly thanks to winds blowing in from the east. In general though, the city enjoys a cool and humid climate with an average summer temperature of around 23°C as well as the occasional heatwave. Spring and autumn are often lovely seasons.

What's new

Veganism is nothing new, of course. But the gusto with which Berlin's currywurst slingers, pho boilers and doughnut shapers have adopted the all-plant ethos is. Whether from a heartfelt commitment to protect the planet or a cynical reach for the city's *green euro*, Berlin has never been so well stocked with vegan restaurants. Fine dining classics like Lucky Leek (see page 84) and old-school veggie-with-vegan-options stalwarts like Brunnenstrasse's Chay Viet (see page 33) have been joined on the scene by newcomers like Brammibal's Donuts (see page 74), where sweet doughy treats come with or without a hole – but always without animal-derived products. Traditional currywurst spots like Konnopke's Imbiss (see page 84) are increasingly popping a decent vegan dog on their menus, and the city's best burger place, Burgermeister (see page 112), has a decent claim on having the best vegan burger in the land.

into West Berlin, while the Soviet zone in the East remained defiantly separate – the city's division was fully realized with the building of the Berlin Wall in August 1961 by the East German government.

The fall of the Wall in 1989 provided a rare opportunity for a late twentieth-century rebirth. Berlin still carries an unfinished air and change remains an exciting constant in the city, though it's not without its growing pains, with gentrification a red-hot topic: Prenzlauer Berg and Mitte have been yuppified beyond

recognition, while in Friedrichshain, Kreuzberg and Neukölln cars are torched, windows smashed in and hip cafés spray-painted with graffiti in an effort to resist.

Political forces and ideals continue to battle it out in Berlin, rendering the city a vibrant and vertiginous place to be: an irresistible combination of entrepreneurial possibility and creative energy rubbing shoulders with a fully developed tourist destination overflowing with museums, sights and events. What's not to like?

Hackesche Höfe Kino

Where to...

Shop

Berlin's fashion scene has been going from strength to strength in the past decade or so, with a string of local designers constantly upping the ante. The city is awash with small boutiques, with clusters around Neue Schönhauser Strasse and Münzstrasse in Spandauer Vorstadt (Mitte) and between Kantstrasse and Ku'damm in Charlottenburg, while Kreuzberg and Friedrichshain have a surfeit of street fashion stores. More commercial shopping can be found around Hackescher Markt and along Ku'damm.
OUR FAVOURITES: do you read me? see page 32. Mall of Berlin see page 52. Bikini Berlin see page 126.

Eat

The dining scene in Berlin has come on leaps and bounds since the Wall fell. Cheap eats are abundant all over the city, with snack stalls – *Imbisse* – hawking everything from burgers and *Currywurst* to Asian food. At the other end, you can dine in style at a decent selection of high-end, Michelin-starred spots – particularly in upscale areas such as Unter den Linden, Potsdamer Platz and Charlottenburg. The area in between – mid-priced restaurants – make up the majority of eating options, again all over the city, and vary from authentic and traditional German restaurants to stylish dens of cool.
OUR FAVOURITES: Cocolo see page 111. Katz Orange see page 35. Dada Falafel see page 34

Drink

The majority of bars are independent, and relaxed licensing laws mean they can usually close when they like. Though there are a decent spread of bars everywhere, the biggest concentration is around Mitte, Prenzlauer Berg, Kreuzberg and Neukölln, with many operating as cafés during the day serving snacks and light meals, and then as bars later on, staying open all the way through to the early hours. Increasingly, young Berliners do their drinking at the city's *spätis* – late-opening convenience stores where the shopkeeper opens your (very affordable) bottle of beer for you to enjoy on a trestle table out front.
OUR FAVOURITES: Schwarze Traube see page 113. Zyankali Bar see page 107. Vagabund Brauerei see page 88

Party

Berlin's nightlife scene is the envy of, well, most of the world, and its large creative scene means that people have fairly flexible schedules. The city's nightclubs not only stay open later than most (some don't close for days) but also purvey some of the most cutting-edge house and techno around, attracting clubbers from around the globe who come to the city just to party the weekend away at heavyweight places like *Berghain/Panorama Bar* and *Watergate*. There's a strong concentration of clubs in Friedrichshain and Kreuzberg.
OUR FAVOURITES: Berghain/Panorama Bar see page 98. Clärchens Ballhaus see page 39. Watergate see page 115

Berlin at a glance

WEDDING

Spandauer Vorstadt p.26.
Dense with boutiques, bars
and restaurants, this is the
heart of Berlin's Mitte district.

**Unter den Linden and the
government quarter** p.46.
Berlin's grandest boulevard
culminates in the imposing
Brandenburg Gate and Reichstag.

Museum
Naturkur

MOABIT

Hauptbahnhof

CHARLOTTENBURG

Reichs

Charlottenburg p.120.
Chic West Berlin, with Ku'damm, Schloss
Charlottenburg, the Zoo and Kaiser-
Wilhelm-Gedächtnis-Kirche.

Brandenburg
Gate

T i e r g a r t e n

Sony
Center

POTSDAM
PLATZ

Kulturforum

Potsdamer Platz and Tiergarten p.64.
Commercial Potsdamer Platz borders the
vast Tiergarten and the Kulturforum, home
to galleries and the Berlin Philharmonic.

SCHÖNEBERG

West Kreuzberg p.100.
Bohemian quarter with a
few major sights – Checkpoir
Charlie and the Jewish Muse
among them.

Schöneberg p.132.
Residential neighbourhood
with a low-key charm.

Prenzlauer Berg and Wedding p.76.
Prenzlauer Berg appeals thanks to its leafy squares filled with cafés and boutiques. Neighbouring Wedding has an edgier sort of charm.

PRENZLAUER BERG

Gedenkstätte
Berliner Mauer

Alexanderplatz and the Nikolaiviertel p.56.
The main square of old East Berlin and neighbouring Nikolaiviertel, a reconstruction of a medieval quarter.

SPANDAUER
VORSTADT

Neue
Synagoge

Hackesche
Höfe

Volkspark
Friedrichshain

ALEXANDER-
PLATZ

Friedrichschain p.90.
East Berlin district that's home to an alternative bars and club scene.

Pergamon-
museum

Fernsehturm

UNTER
EN LINDEN

NIKOLAIVIERTEL

Nikolaikirche

FRIEDRICHSHAIN

MUSEUM
ISLAND

Ostbahnhof

East Side Gallery

Checkpoint
Charlie

The Museum Island p.40.
Five world-class museums, impressively renovated and housing collections of art and antiquities.

WEST
KREUZBERG

Jewish
Museum
Berlin

EAST
KREUZBERG

Kottbusser
Tor

East Kreuzberg p.108.
The more counter-cultural half of Kreuzberg, with a series of superb independent bars.

Neukölln p.116.
Berlin's fastest-changing district is a hipster haven of bars, galleries, cafés and lots of buzz.

NEUKÖLLN

15

Things not to miss

It's not possible to see everything that Berlin has to offer in one trip – and we don't suggest you try. What follows is a selective taste of the city's highlights, from eye-catching architecture to exceptional art.

> **Berliner Fernsehturm**
See page 56
Buy an online fast track ticket to beat the queues and better enjoy the peerless city views from this Berlin landmark.

< **Gemäldegalerie**
See page 65
The undisputed heavyweight of the Kulturforum boasts hundreds of exquisite Old Masters.

∨ **Memorial to the Murdered Jews of Europe**
See page 50
Nineteen thousand square metres of dramatic, disorienting concrete stelae, plus a highly emotive underground museum.

< Hamburger Bahnhof
See page 31
This former train station now houses Berlin's largest collection of cutting-edge international art.

∨ Jewish Museum
See page 103
Daniel Libeskind's Jewish Museum is notable not only for its content but also for its architectural prowess.

< **Reichstag**
See page 50
Having survived fascism, revolution, bombardment and neglect, today the Reichstag is a symbol of the city's reunification.

∨ **Schloss Charlottenburg**
See page 124
The largest palace in Berlin is also a fine example of Prussian-era architecture, built in stunning Rococo and Baroque style.

∧ Gedenkstätte Berliner Mauer
See page 76
The Wall memorial on Bernauer Strasse has fascinating free indoor and outdoor exhibitions.

< Berliner Dom
See page 40
The interior of Berlin's neo-Renaissance cathedral is as dramatic as its outsized exterior.

∧ Panoramapunkt
See page 65

Take a high-speed ride to the top of the Art Deco Kollhoff Tower for soaring vistas over Potsdamer Platz and beyond.

∨ Deutsches Technikmuseum
See page 101

A jaw-dropping ensemble of German technical innovations, past and present.

∧ **Topography of Terror**
See page 101
Located where the SS headquarters used to be, this museum unflinchingly explores the rise of the Nazi party and its atrocities.

< **Museum Island**
See page 40
A treasure trove of ancient and modern art spread over five world-class museums.

‹ Brandenburger Tor
See page 49
One of Berlin's most iconic landmarks and the site of many major historical events.

⌄ East Side Gallery
See page 91
This significant remaining stretch of the Berlin Wall doubles as one of the world's longest open-air art galleries.

Day one in Berlin

Breakfast. See page 55. Coffee and a pastry at an *Einstein café* is the thinking person's way to start the day in Berlin. The Unter den Linden outpost is a favourite.

Museum Island. See page 40. Admire the stunning architectural array and explore five fantastic museums on an island in the Spree, the historic centre of the city.

Neue Wache. See page 46. Visit SchinkVel's famous Neoclassical monument and its moving tributes to victims of wartime, including the emotive Käthe Kollwitz sculpture *Mother with her Dead Son*.

Deutsches Historisches Museum

Lunch For a tasty budget option in the area try sushi at *Ishin* (see page 54); for classic Austro-German dishes opt for *Lutter & Wegner* (see page 54).

Brandenburg Gate. See page 49. Berlin's foremost landmark and one of its biggest tourist attractions. A must-see for first-time visitors after a leisurely stroll down Unter den Linden.

Reichstag. See page 50. Climb the Norman Foster-designed dome of this historic building to enjoy great views across the city. Make sure you book a guided tour ahead of time.

Brandenburg Gate location

Memorial to the Murdered Jews of Europe. See page 50. Visit the controversial memorial with its rows of stelae above ground and sobering visitor centre below.

Dinner. See page 53. End the day with some quality European-nouveau meat or fish dishes and fine service at *Crackers*.

Reichstag

Day two in Berlin

Breakfast. See page 131. West Berlin's *Schwarzes Café* is a vaguely bohemian 24-hour café with a relaxed, spacious interior upstairs (more of a "Black Café" downstairs) and decent breakfasts.

Berlin Zoo and Aquarium. See page 120. One of the biggest zoos in Europe – hippos are among the celebrated residents – with an equally comprehensive aquarium right around the corner.

Kaiser-Wilhelm-Gedächtnis-Kirche. See page 121. Nicknamed "the hollow tooth" for its shattered spire, damaged in a 1943 air raid, this memorial church has a wonderful interior to investigate.

Käthe Kollwitz Museum. See page 124. The biggest collection of work from Berlin's pre-eminent sculptor displayed in a lovely villa in the grounds of Schloss Charlottenburg.

Lunch. See page 129. Grab a casual lunch at *Lon Men's Noodle House*, a simple yet thriving Taiwanese noodle spot.

Shopping on Ku'damm. See page 126. Since you're near the mighty Kurfürstendamm it'd be a shame not to indulge in some retail therapy. Don't forget to check the side streets too for a host of excellent, independent boutiques.

Dinner. See pages 128 and 129. Try some thoroughly old-fashioned Silesian and Pomeranian food at *Marjellchen*, a marvellous time warp. Or head to *893 Ryotei* for cutting edge Japanese food with Mexican and Peruvian twists.

Berlin Zoo

Kaiser-Wilhelm-Gedächtnis-Kirche

Käthe Kollwitz Museum

GDR Berlin

Take an "Ostalgie" tour through former East Berlin, its monumental sights, kitsch icons and memorials to the city's divided past.

DDR Museum. See page 57. Get hands on with GDR culture at this interactive museum, which evokes both the lighter and darker sides of life in communist East Germany. Nearby stand statues of Marx and Engels, tucked into a corner of the Marx-Engels-Forum park.

Berliner Fernsehturm. See page 56. Gape at the austere GDR architecture of Alexanderplatz before taking a trip up the Fernsehturm for tremendous views over the city.

Lunch. See page 57. For the complete television tower experience, book ahead for a meal in the revolving restaurant, *Sphere*.

Karl-Marx-Allee. See page 91. Admire the Soviet architecture along this impressive historical boulevard, formerly known as Stalinallee, including the original Kino International, as featured in the film *Good Bye Lenin!*

Coffee. See page 96. Grab coffee and cake (or ice cream) at *Café Sybille*, which also hosts a small but informative museum about Karl-Marx-Allee.

East Side Gallery. See page 91. Finish up at the largest remaining section of the Berlin Wall, also one of the world's largest open-air galleries.

DDR Museum

Café Sybille

Karl Marx Allee

Budget Berlin

Berlin's not necessarily an expensive city, and there are plenty of fun ways to explore on the cheap.

Breakfast. See page 87. Tuck into the weekend vegan breakfast at *Morgenrot* in Prenzlauer Berg, a collective-run café, one of the best value places in town.

Take the bus. See page 153. Public buses #100 and #200 will give you a guided tour of some of the city's main sights at a fraction of the cost of marketed tour buses.

Lunch. See pages 34 and 73. *Joseph Roth Diele*, a charming restaurant near Potsdamer Platz, is dedicated to the Jewish author and has excellent lunch deals. If you're after a quick fix you can't go wrong with a falafel at *Dada Falafel*.

Topography of Terror. See page 101. Built on the grounds of the former SS Headquarters, this memorial of Gestapo horrors will leave you reeling.

Gedenkstätte Berliner Mauer. See page 76. The Wall memorial on Bernauer Strasse has fascinating indoor and outdoor exhibitions for free.

Drinks. See page 38. Drink and make merry at one of the *Weinerei* bars, low-key, hipster hangouts that pride themselves on their reasonable prices.

Museum of Things

Joseph Roth Diele

Drinking at Weinerei Forum

Berlin nightlife

Berlin's nightlife is justifiably renowned around the globe, with several distinct nightlife districts making it easy to spend an evening – or even an entire weekend – exploring the city's multitude of bars and clubs.

Clärchens Ballhaus. See page 39. Start the night with a pretzel and Pilsner at this charming century-old dance hall, which hosts a variety of nights from Tango to classical concerts.

B-Flat. See page 39. One of the most dynamic jazz spots in the city, with regular international guests and weekly jam sessions.

Schokoladen. See page 39. For more live music, head to intimate Schokoladen which hosts upcoming rock and punk acts in a bare brick (former squat, former chocolate factory) interior.

Interior of Clärchens Ballhaus

Club der Visionaere. See page 112. A top pre-club spot, CdV has the advantage of being mostly set outdoors on a floating deck. The dancefloor is small, but the vibes can be big on the right night.

Renate. See page 99. One of the most reliably fun nightspots in the city, the parties have an arty aesthetic and favour a house and disco soundtrack over the usual techno.

Berghain/Panorama Bar. See page 98. Whether you'll get in or not is notoriously difficult to predict, but if you can penetrate Berlin's world-famous techno temple you'll realise why it's considered one of the best in the world. The Saturday night party runs until Monday morning.

The Tempodrom

Tempodrom. See page 107. Hailed as a concrete circus, this giant big-top tent is the perfect place to see live music. It has seen the likes of Björk and Blur grace its stage. It also hosts operas, orchestras, comedy acts, circus artists, and so much more.

Renate

Open spaces

Although it's known more for its urban thrills, the German capital is a surprisingly green city. Its many parks often come with plenty of options for activities (jogging, volleyball, barbecues, rowing on lakes), along with lots of history.

Mauerpark. See page 76. Salvaged by local residents after the fall of the Wall, this scruffy but popular park was once the Wall's "death strip" between East and West Berlin. Visit on a Sunday to find life-affirming public karaoke and a popular flea market.

Viktoriapark. See page 104. This much-loved Kreuzberg park is famous for having the tallest peak in the city. It also offers a pretty waterfall in summer and lots of hills for winter sledging.

Tiergarten. See page 71. The city's most famous park used to be a hunting ground for the Kaiser and his cohorts. Nowadays it provides ample running and walking tracks, lakes and a couple of great beer gardens.

Tempelhofer Park. See page 104. One of the largest and most unique parks in Europe, this former Nazi airport is now a vast community space where residents and visitors can rollerblade and kitesurf along the former runway.

Volkspark Friedrichshain. See page 90. GDR-era memorials abound at this sprawling city park, which also offers a picturesque nineteenth-century fountain, a great recreational area with climbing walls and sandy volleyball courts, and a couple of beer gardens.

Pfaueninsel. See page 140. Take to the water to escape the city for a fantasy island getaway. A car-free nature reserve stalked by a flock of peacocks, Pfaueninsel also features a mini-Schloss and gardens landscaped by the original designer of the Tiergarten.

Mauerpark

Viktoriapark

Tempelhof Park

PLACES

The Reichstag

DEM DEUTSCHEN VOLKE

Spandauer Vorstadt

Arcing elegantly above the Spree between Friedrichstrasse and Alexanderplatz, the Spandauer Vorstadt was an eighteenth-century suburb that today serves as Berlin's primary "downtown" area and is the heart of the Mitte district. Before World War II it was a significant hub for Jewish and French Huguenot exiles; after the Wall fell it became an artists' enclave, playing a vital role in the transferral of the city's art scene from West to East. Three decades of commercialization have resulted in a vibrant but touristic part of the city that's dense with boutiques, bars and restaurants, mainly around Hackescher Markt and the adjacent Oranienburger Strasse, as well as galleries along Auguststrasse and Torstrasse. Key insights into local Jewish life remain at the Neue Synagoge, the Jewish cemetery on Grosse Hamburger Strasse and two museums in the Haus Schwarzenberg.

Hackesche Höfe

MAP PAGE 28, POCKET MAP E12
Rosenthaler Str. 40/41 & Sophienstr. 6
Ⓢ Hackescher Markt Ⓦ hackesche-hoefe.com.

The extensive series of interconnected courtyards known as the Hackesche Höfe, located just across from S-Bahn station **Hackescher Markt**, are one of the best-known sights in this area. Having formerly hosted a Jewish girls' club, ballroom, factories, apartments – even a poets' society – the courtyards were remixed post-Wall into a more commercial enterprise, albeit with a vaguely arty twist. Today you'll find a cinema, several theatres, a jumble of smart restaurants and shops – and a throng of tourists, attracted by the impressive **Art Nouveau** restoration.

Haus Schwarzenberg

MAP PAGE 28, POCKET MAP E12
Rosenthaler Str. 39 Ⓢ Hackescher Markt
Ⓦ haus-schwarzenberg.org.

Haus Schwarzenberg is the grungy alternative to gentrified Hackesche Höfe, located just a couple of doors away. It has only been minimally refurbished and at least part of its allure is its wonderful crumbling facades. Inside is an aptly unpretentious selection of cafés, bars and shops plus a cinema and galleries (street-art lovers will want to visit Neurotitan Gallery), as well as the **Monsterkabinett**, a collection of moving mechanical monsters (Ⓦ monsterkabinett.de; charge). Of particular interest are two small museums that explore Jewish life in the area and beyond during the Third Reich. One focuses on Otto Weidt, a German entrepreneur who helped save a number of his blind Jewish employees, hiding them in his workshop. Now called the **Museum Blindenwerkstatt Otto Weidt** (Ⓦ museum-blindenwerkstatt.de; free), it preserves photographs and personal mementoes of Weidt and his workers and the claustrophobic, hidden room, located behind a backless wardrobe, where he hid Jewish families when the Gestapo came knocking. The **Anne-Frank-Zentrum** (Ⓦ annefrank.de; charge) is a modern, engaging exhibition on her life.

Sammlung Hoffmann

MAP PAGE 28, POCKET MAP D11
Sophie-Gips-Höfe, Sophienstr. 21
Ⓢ Hackescher Markt Ⓦ sammlung-hoffmann.de. By appointment only; charge.

Started by avid art collectors Erika and Rolf Hoffmann, this sizeable private museum displays their personal collection of contemporary art, which spans painting, sculpture, photography and video over two floors filled with natural light. Organized subjectively – there are no names, descriptions or over-arching curatorial themes – the exhibition features internationally renowned names such as **Jean-Michel Basquiat**, **Andy Warhol** and **Bruce Nauman**. The collection is rearranged every year. Entry

is by guided tour (English tours available) – a pleasantly interactive and informative way of experiencing such major works.

Neue Synagoge

MAP PAGE 28, POCKET MAP D12
Oranienburger Str. 28–30 Ⓢ Oranienburger Str. Ⓦ centrumjudaicum.de. Charge.

Topped with a golden, glittering dome that almost rivals the Reichstag's for prowess and recognition, the Moorish Neue Synagoge (New Synagogue) is a building with a long and largely brutal history. Consecrated on Rosh Hashanah in 1866, it quickly became the **most important synagogue in Berlin**; in its prime it could house over three thousand worshippers. Its fortunes changed under the Nazis and the synagogue was heavily vandalized during *Kristallnacht* (1938), bombed by Allied planes (1945) and demolished by the GDR in the 1950s. Rebuilt and restored in the 1990s, it stands

Neue Synagoge

Spandauer Vorstadt

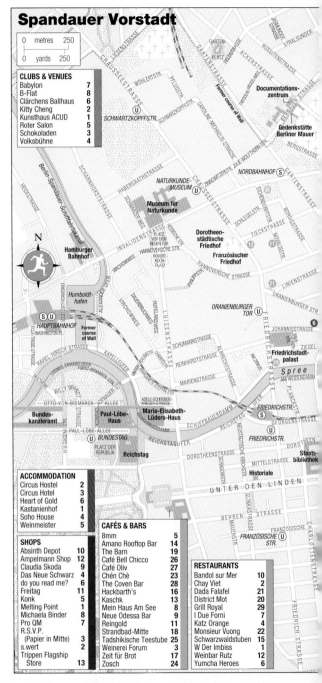

| 0 | metres | 250 |
| 0 | yards | 250 |

CLUBS & VENUES

Babylon	7
B-Flat	8
Clärchens Ballhaus	6
Kitty Cheng	2
Kunsthaus ACUD	1
Roter Salon	5
Schokoladen	3
Volksbühne	4

ACCOMMODATION

Circus Hostel	2
Circus Hotel	3
Heart of Gold	6
Kastanienhof	1
Soho House	4
Weinmeister	5

SHOPS

Absinth Depot	10
Ampelmann Shop	12
Claudia Skoda	9
Das Neue Schwarz	4
do you read me?	1
Freitag	11
Konk	5
Melting Point	8
Michaela Binder	8
Pro QM	7
R.S.V.P. (Papier in Mitte)	3
s.wert	2
Trippen Flagship Store	13

CAFÉS & BARS

8mm	5
Amano Rooftop Bar	14
The Barn	19
Café Bell Chicco	26
Café Oliv	27
Chén Chè	23
The Coven Bar	28
Hackbarth's	16
Kaschk	13
Mein Haus Am See	8
Neue Odessa Bar	9
Reingold	11
Strandbad-Mitte	18
Tadshikische Teestube	3
Weinerei Forum	3
Zeit für Brot	17
Zosch	24

RESTAURANTS

Bandol sur Mer	10
Chay Viet	2
Dada Falafel	21
District Mot	20
Grill Royal	29
I Due Forni	7
Katz Orange	4
Monsieur Vuong	22
Schwarzwaldstuben	15
W Der Imbiss	1
Weinbar Rutz	12
Yumcha Heroes	6

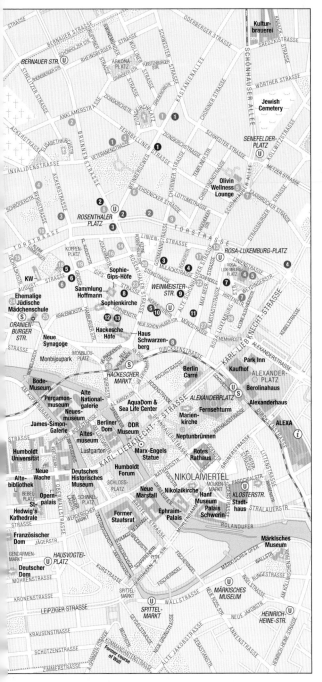

Friedrichstadt-Palast at night

proudly today both as a memorial to Jewish suffering in Germany and a depository of local Jewish culture. Sadly it wasn't possible to restore all of the synagogue and its interior, so the front section (or **Centrum Judaicum**) displays the oldest surviving elements – original carvings, entrance vestibules and anterooms – and hosts exhibitions, which mostly focus on the history of the building and Jewish Berlin. You can get an idea of the building's former dimensions by visiting a gravel-covered area outside, which marks the original layout of the synagogue.

KW Institute for Contemporary Art

MAP PAGE 28, POCKET MAP D11
Auguststr. 69 Ⓢ Oranienburger Str. Ⓦ kw-berlin.de. Charge.

The KW Institute for Contemporary Art was one of the prime movers in the post-*Wende* (reunification) transformation of Auguststrasse into what has been dubbed Berlin's **"art mile"**. Once a nineteenth-century margarine factory, KW was turned into

a dedicated art space by Klaus Biesenbach and a group of fellow art lovers in the early 1990s. The elegant facade leads into a lovely, tree-filled courtyard surrounded by artist studios, the glass-walled *Café Bravo* (designed by American artist Dan Graham) and a series of modern, white spaces that include an exhibition hall by Berlin architect Hans Düttmann. The institute mainly exhibits cutting-edge international works from both up-and-coming and major names such as Doug Aitken, Dinos and Jake Chapman and Paul Pfeiffer. KW also runs Berlin's immensely popular **Biennale for Contemporary Art**.

Ehemalige Jüdische Mädchenschule

MAP PAGE 28, POCKET MAP D11
Auguststr. 11–13 Ⓢ Oranienburger Str. Ⓦ maedchenschule.org.

Built in the late 1920s as one of the last major Jewish structures before the Nazis took over, this charming former Jewish girls' school opened as a space for **art and cuisine** in 2012 following a sensitive restoration. The former classrooms and corridors are now used for cultural venues such as the Rooftop Playground and Michael Fuchs galleries, and Museum Frieder Burda's Salon Berlin, an offshoot of the modern art museum in Baden-Baden. As for cuisine, *House of Small Wonder* is a Japanese-American café serving excellent breakfasts and izakaya-style dishes at dinner.

Friedrichstadt-Palast

MAP PAGE 28, POCKET MAP C12
Friedrichstr. 107 ⑤ Friedrichstr. ⓦ palast.
berlin.

Founded in the 1860s, this **theatre** has a long and distinguished history, having been a market hall, circus, theatre and, during the Nazi era, the Theater des Volkes, when it staged bourgeois operettas. Its current incarnation – an imposing GDR-style block – was opened in 1984. The stage is a whopping 2800 square metres and the main hall holds up to two thousand people for its programme of revue shows.

Museum für Naturkunde

MAP PAGE 28, POCKET MAP A10
Invalidenstr. 43 ⓤ Naturekundemuseum
ⓦ naturkundemuseum-berlin.de. Charge.

Inaugurated in 1889 by Emperor Wilhelm II, Berlin's natural history museum is the largest of its kind in Germany, counting some thirty million objects within its collections. Highlights include the largest mounted dinosaur in the world – a *Brachiosaurus brancai* composed of fossilized bones – plus a 2015 T. Rex skeleton found in Montana and an impressive room of stuffed animals that showcase biodiversity.

Hamburger Bahnhof

MAP PAGE 28, POCKET MAP A11
Invalidenstr. 50 ⑤/ⓤ Hauptbahnhof
ⓦ smb.museum. Charge.

Occupying a capacious and architecturally interesting space (formerly one of the city's first terminal stations), Berlin's contemporary art museum (Museum für Gegenwart) is one of the city's major modern art venues. Its permanent collection, which features holdings from the Nationalgalerie, focuses on the major movements of the late twentieth century up to the present day, with an emphasis on installation art and a number of large-scale sculptures by conceptual artists such as Joseph Beuys. The museum's **Marx Collection** has works by Anselm Kiefer and Andy Warhol, while Friedrich Christian Flick's collection, donated in 2004, added works by artists like Isa Genzken, Bruce Nauman, Pipilotti Rist and Wolfgang Tillmans. The museum also hosts temporary exhibitions by international artists at the forefront of their respective fields.

Hamburger Bahnhof

Shops

Absinth Depot

MAP PAGE 28, POCKET MAP E11
Weinmeisterstr. 4 ⓤ Weinmeisterstr.
ⓦ absinthdepot.de.

The place not only to find all kinds of "Green Fairy" liquor but also a wide variety of props for the true absinth experience. You can even have a little taste.

Ampelmann Shop

MAP PAGE 28, POCKET MAP D11
Rosenthaler Str. 40–41 ⓤ Weinmeisterstr.
ⓦ ampelmann.de.

Everything here is based on the Ampelmännchen – the distinctive (and stylish) traffic light men once present on all East German traffic lights, who were saved from extinction after the Wall fell by various high-profile campaigns.

Claudia Skoda

MAP PAGE 28, POCKET MAP E11
Alte Schönhauser Str. 35 ⓤ Weinmeisterstr.
ⓦ claudiaskoda.com.

Skoda's renowned knitwear is unapologetically chic (and correspondingly expensive). The clothes are geared mostly for women but there's a small men's section too.

Das Neue Schwarz

MAP PAGE 28, POCKET MAP E11
Mulackstr. 38 ⓤ Weinmeisterstr. ⓦ www.
dasneueschwarz.de.

"The New Black" stocks vintage designer garments for men and women. Expect handbags, shoes, suits and jackets from top designer brands.

do you read me?

MAP PAGE 28, POCKET MAP D11
Auguststr. 28 ⓤ Rosenthaler Platz ⓦ www.
doyoureadme.de.

A magazine lover's paradise, this multilingual store offers a vast assortment of magazines and reading material from around the world, covering fashion and photography, art and architecture, culture and literature.

Freitag

MAP PAGE 28, POCKET MAP E11
Max-Beer-Str. 3 ⓤ/Ⓢ Alexanderplatz
ⓦ www.freitag.ch.

The Mitte flagship store features concrete, couches and catwalk lighting – all of which provides the perfect backdrop for Markus Freitag's creations: thousands of colourful, durable bags in every shape imaginable.

Konk

MAP PAGE 28, POCKET MAP D11
Kleine Hamburger Str. 15 Ⓢ Oranienburger
Str. ⓦ konk-berlin.de.

Featuring collections from many of Berlin's esteemed labels (Anntian, Boessert/Schorn, Marina Hoermannseder), this boutique features cutting-edge fashions, jewellery and other glamorous accessories that flit between fashion and art.

Melting Point

MAP PAGE 28, POCKET MAP E10
Kastanienallee 55 ⓤ Rosenthaler Platz
ⓣ 030 44 04 71 31.

Opened in the mid-1990s, this popular record store has stayed true to Berlin's techno and house scene, though it also sells funk, disco, soul and more.

Michaela Binder

MAP PAGE 28, POCKET MAP E11
Gipsstr. 13 ⓤ Weinmeisterstr.
ⓦ michaelabinder.de.

Michaela Binder's smart shop stocks her stylish rings, bracelets, ear studs and necklaces in clean, basic shapes, from silver and gold. There's also a line of (cheaper) steel and stone vases.

Pro QM

MAP PAGE 28, POCKET MAP F11
Almstadtstr. 48 ⓤ Rosa-Luxemburg-Platz
ⓦ pro-qm.de.

Run by an artist and an architecture professor, this smart

and surprisingly spacious store specializes in books and magazines dedicated to these subjects, as well as design and craft, and spans lifestyle as well as academic publications.

R.S.V.P. (Papier in Mitte)

MAP PAGE 28, POCKET MAP E11
Mulackstr. 14 ⓤ Weinmeisterstr. Ⓦ rsvp-berlin.de.

From rare international notebooks to the store's own unique cards and journals, R.S.V.P. sells elegant stationery and related products from international artists. A shop at no. 26 sells wrapping paper, boxes and envelopes.

s.wert

MAP PAGE 28, POCKET MAP D10
Brunnenstr. 191 ⓤ Rosenthaler Platz
Ⓦ s.wert.de.

Interested in special Berliner "architecture pillows", or unique designs of wrapping paper? s.wert sells all this and more, including stylish drinking cups, dresses and curtains.

Trippen Flagship Store

MAP PAGE 28, POCKET MAP D11

Hackesche Höfe, Hofs 4 & 6, Rosenthaler Str. 40/41 Ⓢ Hackescher Markt. Ⓦ trippen.com.

Trippen sells men's and women's shoes for every occasion. There are several branches around, but this flagship store has the best range. Footwear also made to order.

Restaurants

Bandol sur Mer

MAP PAGE 28, POCKET MAP D11
Torstr. 167 ⓤ Rosenthaler Platz
Ⓦ bandolsurmer.de.

A former kebab kiosk refurbished into a tiny, Michelin-starred French restaurant serving a seasonal tasting menu. The sister restaurant next door, 3 minutes sur mer (Ⓦ 3minutessurmer.de), is a more casual brasserie-style affair. €€€€

Chay Viet

MAP PAGE 28, POCKET MAP D10
Brunnenstr. 164 ⓤ Rosenthaler Platz
Ⓦ chay-viet-restaurant.eatbu.com.

There's a lot of great Vietnamese food in Berlin, and there's a lot of great vegan food too… but this might just be the best iteration of

Ampelmann T-shirts for sale

Bandol sur Mer

both. The food is flavourful, the menu is inventive, and you'll get a square meal for less than €16. The noodle soups will wow you – especially the Mi Quang. €

Dada Falafel

MAP PAGE 28, POCKET MAP C11
Linienstr. 132 Ⓤ Oranienburger Tor
Ⓦ dadafalafel.de.
Berlin isn't exactly short of falafels, but *Dada* stands out thanks to their fresh salads and an excellent array of sauces. The Dada Teller will set you up for a day's sightseeing, though expect long queues at lunchtimes. €

District Mot

MAP PAGE 28, POCKET MAP E11
Rosenthaler Str. 62 Ⓤ Rosenthaler Platz
Ⓦ district-mot.com.
A Vietnamese street food restaurant, serving dishes you would find on the streets of Saigon, such as *Cá Kho Tho* (braised Mekong fish in caramel sauce) or *Chân Gà Nuong* (grilled chicken

feet) for more adventurous eaters. Décor is typical Vietnamese street food style: simple with stools and chopsticks all ready to go in a bowl on the table. €€

Grill Royal

MAP PAGE 28, POCKET MAP C12
Friedrichstr. 105b Ⓤ Oranienburger Tor
Ⓦ grillroyal.com.
The steaks are definitely high end at this celeb-friendly restaurant. Some of the best Argentine, German, French and Japanese cuts in town are served, as well as excellent seafood and wines. In summer try and reserve a seat out on the Spree-facing terrace. €€€€

I Due Forni

MAP PAGE 28, POCKET MAP F10
Schönhauser Allee 12 Ⓤ Senefelderplatz
Ⓣ 030 44 01 73 33.
This famous Italian joint serves up cheap and tasty brick-oven pizzas and pasta dishes, in an idiosyncratic atmosphere, aided by the punk staff (all Italian) and – in summer

– a large beer garden. Service is appropriately blasé. €€

Katz Orange

MAP PAGE 28, POCKET MAP D10
Bergstr. 22 ⓤ/Ⓢ Nordbahnhof
ⓦ katzorange.com.

Tucked away in a restored, nineteenth-century brewery in Mitte, the (slightly) glamorous "orange cat" offers a pleasant blend of casual and fine dining with an international menu that runs from salads to quality fish and meat dishes. There's also a cocktail bar and a lovely courtyard terrace for warmer weather. €€€€

Monsieur Vuong

MAP PAGE 28, POCKET MAP E11
Alte Schönhauser Str. 46 ⓤ Rosa-Luxemburg-Platz ⓦ monsieurvuong.de.

The light, simple and cheap Vietnamese food served at *Monsieur Vuong* has made it one of the most popular dining spots in Mitte. The menu changes every few days but there's always good fresh soups, noodle salads and fruit cocktails. You may have to wait for a table, especially at peak times. €€€

Schwarzwaldstuben

MAP PAGE 28, POCKET MAP C11
Tucholskystr. 48 Ⓢ Oranienburger Str.
ⓦ schwarzwaldstuben.berlin.

This Mitte mainstay doubles as a casual restaurant serving hearty Swabian food – think Sauerkraut, *Maultaschen* (filled pasta) and *Flammkuchen* (a type of thin-crust pizza) – and a friendly bar in the evenings with decent German beers on draught. €€

W Der Imbiss

MAP PAGE 28, POCKET MAP H2
Kastanienallee 49 ⓤ Senefelderplatz
☎ 030 43 35 22 06.

Easily identified by its cheekily inverted *McDonald's* sign, *Imbiss W* serves up fusion food that includes such unusual items as naan pizza and other bright ideas. The results can be a bit hit and miss, but they're generally good and reasonably priced, with an emphasis on veggie/vegan eats. €€

Weinbar Rutz

MAP PAGE 28, POCKET MAP B11
Chausseestr. 8 ⓤ Naturkundemuseum
ⓦ rutz-restaurant.de.

Triple-Michelin-starred cuisine on the second floor and over eight hundred wines on offer make this a de rigueur stop for foodies. It's expensive, but it's one of the best destination dining venues in the city. €€€€

Yumcha Heroes

MAP PAGE 28, POCKET MAP E16
Weinbergsweg 8 ⓤ Rosenthaler Platz
ⓦ yumchaheroes.de.

With the same owners as nearby Portuguese café *Galao*, *Yumcha Heroes* is *the* place in Mitte for dumplings – steamed, baked or in a tasty broth. The food is handmade, cooked in an open kitchen and served in a small but stylish interior. €€

District Mot

Cafés and bars

8mm

MAP PAGE 28, POCKET MAP F10
Schönhauser Allee 177b Ⓤ Senefelderplatz
Ⓦ 8mmbar.com.
It's just a small, blacked-out room
with a small bar, a DJ spinning
anything from rock to northern
soul and 8mm films projected onto
one wall – but it's a superb place
for low-key, late-night hedonism.

Amano Rooftop Bar

MAP PAGE 28, POCKET MAP E11
Auguststr. 43 Ⓤ Rosenthaler Platz Ⓦ www.
amanogroup.de.
The rooftop bar at the *Amano*
hotel has become a firm summer
favourite, not only for the see-and-
be-seen ambience and views across
Mitte's rooftops but also for its
excellent array of summery wines
and cocktails.

Hackbarth's

The Barn

MAP PAGE 28, POCKET MAP D11
Auguststr. 58 Ⓤ Rosenthaler Platz
Ⓦ thebarn.de.
Wooden shelves stacked with
delicious products for sale, some
of the best coffee in town, homemade cakes and sandwiches using
bread from local artisan bakeries
all make *The Barn* well worth a
visit. They also have a spacious
roastery-café in Prenzlauer Berg
(Schönhauser Allee 8) and a
couple of other locations in the
city. €

Café Bell Chicco

MAP PAGE 28, POCKET MAP F12
Rosa-Luxemburg-Str. 16 Ⓤ /
Ⓢ Alexanderplatz Ⓦ bellchicco.de.
Elegant little café serving great
coffee, homemade cakes and
delicious brunches in a cosy and
welcoming sunny yellow room. €

Café Oliv

MAP PAGE 28, POCKET MAP E12
Münzstr. 8 Ⓤ Weinmeisterstrasse Ⓦ oliv-
cafe.de.
With a modern interior, great
coffee and decent, unpretentious
food (sandwiches, quiches, soups,
cakes), this is a pleasant spot
for breakfast or lunch, and very
convenient for a respite from
boutique shopping. €

Chén Chè

MAP PAGE 28, POCKET MAP E11
Rosenthaler Str. 13 Ⓤ Rosenthaler Platz
Ⓦ chenche-berlin.de.
This charming Vietnamese
tearoom, with its high ceilings
and elegant, handmade lanterns,
has a small but considered menu
featuring a selection of starters
and mains as well as great teas and
coffees. Try one of the weekend
breakfasts for something a bit
different. €

The Coven Bar

MAP PAGE 28, POCKET MAP H2
Kleine Präsidenten Str. 3 Ⓢ Hackescher
Markt. Ⓦ thecovenberlin.com.

Amano Rooftop Bar

Well-designed, uber-modern bar serving craft cocktails. The service is friendly and the atmosphere relaxed: there are few better ways to end your evening in this area.

Hackbarth's

MAP PAGE 28, POCKET MAP D11
Auguststr. 49a Ⓤ Rosenthaler Platz Ⓣ 030 28 27 704.
With its simple wooden interior and crowd of regulars, *Hackbarth's* is a casually tasteful option. Snacks and freshly baked cakes are offered during the day. €

Kaschk

MAP PAGE 28, POCKET MAP F11
Linienstr. 40 Ⓤ Rosa-Luxemburg-Platz Ⓦ kaschk.de.
This hip place serves top-notch third-wave coffee, a great selection of local and international (especially Nordic) craft beers and – downstairs – Germany's first ever shuffleboards.

Mein Haus Am See

MAP PAGE 28, POCKET MAP D16
Brunnenstr. 197–198 Ⓤ Rosenthaler Platz Ⓦ mein-haus-am-see.club.

A spacious café/bar, stumbling distance from Rosenthaler Platz, *Mein Haus am See* is filled with comfy flea-market furnishings and is as good a spot for reading a book as it is for a drink late at night, when DJs play anything from disco to house and indie.

Neue Odessa Bar

MAP PAGE 28, POCKET MAP E10
Torstr. 89 Ⓤ Rosenthaler Platz/Rosa-Luxemburg-Platz Ⓣ 0171 839 89 91.
Neue Odessa Bar is something of a place-to-be thanks to a well-thought-out combination of attractive, swanky interior, reasonably made cocktails and table service. Perpetually busy.

Reingold

MAP PAGE 28, POCKET MAP C11
Novalisstr. 11 Ⓤ Oranienburger Tor Ⓣ 030 28 38 76 76.
Featuring one of the most impressive bars in town – certainly one of the longest – this classy 1920s-themed watering hole offers impeccably attired waiters who make meticulous cocktails.

Babylon

Strandbad-Mitte

MAP PAGE 28, POCKET MAP D11
Kleine Hamburger Str. 16 ⑤ Oranienburger
Str. ⓦ strandbad-mitte.de.
This laidback café, with breezy,
green-tiled, seaside-themed
decor, is slightly off the tourist
routes and has a correspondingly
local vibe. The food and coffee
and cakes are good and the staff
friendly. €

Tadshikische Teestube

MAP PAGE 28, POCKET MAP D11
Oranienburger Str. 27 ⑤ Oranienburger Str.
ⓦ tadshikische-teestube.de.
This delightful "Tajik Tea Room"
has a stunning cushions-and-
carpets interior, a vast tea menu
and a kids' storyteller on Mondays
spinning fairytales in German.

Weinerei Forum

MAP PAGE 28, POCKET MAP E10
Shop: Veteranenstr. 17; bar: Fehrbellnir Str.
57 ⓤ Rosenthaler Platz ⓦ weinerei.com.
This "underground" members club-
style wine shop used to operate

an honesty box system – but
Covid regulations and pressures
put paid to that. The emphasis is
still on value, and the atmosphere
is friendly. The owners run other
ventures nearby.

Zeit für Brot

MAP PAGE 28, POCKET MAP E11
Alte Schönhauser Str. 4 ⓤ Rosa-
Luxemburg-Platz ⓦ zeitfuerbrot.com.
This café offers a mellow, pastel-
coloured interior, large windows
and an eye-catching assortment
of artisanal breads (you can see
the bakers working away through
a Perspex window). The quiches,
sandwiches and sweets are organic
and delicious. There are other
branches across the city, including
one in Charlottenburg. €

Zosch

MAP PAGE 28, POCKET MAP C11
Tucholskystr. 30 ⓤ Oranienburger Str.
ⓦ zosch-berlin.de.
Alternative place that started as a
squat when the Wall came down

and has retained an early 90s feel. A good place for gigs and club nights in the cellar, where a fun-loving local Creole jazz band often plays amid the smoky ambience and constant chatter.

Clubs and venues

Babylon

MAP PAGE 28, POCKET MAP F11
Rosa-Luxemburg-Str. 30 ⓤ Rosa-Luxemburg-Platz ⓦ babylonberlin.eu.
This striking Berlin *Kino* opened in 1929 and remains one of the defining architectural landmarks of Rosa-Luxemburg-Platz. Today the cinema shows a mix of indie, trash, silents with live organ music and cult movies, as well as hosting concerts and over forty film festivals annually.

B-Flat

MAP PAGE 28, POCKET MAP E11
Dircksenstr. 40 ⓤ Rosenthaler Platz ⓦ b-flat-berlin.de.
This cosy jazz club offers a mix of local musicians and the occasional international act. There's a cheap jam session on Wednesdays.

Clärchens Ballhaus

MAP PAGE 28, POCKET MAP D11
Auguststr. 24 ⓤ Rosenthaler Platz dor Weinmeisterstr. ⓦ ballhaus.de.
This authentic pre-war ballroom still hosts dance classes, but at weekends the downstairs is taken over by one of the most diverse crowds (young, old, straight, gay) in Berlin, drawn by the unique atmosphere of a live covers band and an unpretentious good time. Good snacks and a pleasant garden too.

Kitty Cheng

MAP PAGE 28, POCKET MAP E10
Torstr. 99 ⓤ Rosa-Luxemburg-Platz ⓦ kittycheng.de.
With its vintage theme – red-and-white-striped walls, regal furnishings – and lengthy drinks list, this slightly under-the-radar spot manages to attract the attention of Mitte's buzzy (and spoiled-for-choice) party crowd. The best parties are at the weekend and the music is refreshingly diverse.

Kunsthaus ACUD

MAP PAGE 28, POCKET MAP D10
Veteranenstr. 21 ⓤ Rosenthaler Platz ⓦ acud.de.
One of the few cultural spaces left from the immediate post-Wall era, ACUD contains a theatre, cinema, club, bar and studio, and puts on regular concerts.

Roter Salon

MAP PAGE 28, POCKET MAP F11
Rosa-Luxemburg-Platz 1 ⓤ Rosa-Luxemburg-Platz ⓦ volksbuehne.berlin.
Set within the Volksbühne theatre, this long-running venue's lurid red decor and chintzy furniture give it a 1950s feel. Readings, concerts and talks are held here.

Schokoladen

MAP PAGE 28, POCKET MAP D10
Ackerstr. 169 ⓤ Rosenthaler Platz ⓦ schokoladen-mitte.de.
A small live venue (in a former chocolate factory) that is a bit like visiting a private lounge – albeit one with cheap drinks, a friendly atmosphere and a consistently good line-up of indie and punk bands and upcoming singer-songwriters.

Volksbühne

MAP PAGE 28, POCKET MAP F11
Rosa-Luxemburg-Platz (Linienstrasse 227) ⓤ Rosa-Luxemburg-Platz ⓦ volksbuehne-berlin.de.
Built just before World War I, the Volksbühne ("People's Theatre") has its origin in the free people's theatre movement. Damaged during World War II, it was rebuilt in the 1950s and is now established as one of Germany's most experimental theatres. The venue also hosts club nights and concerts.

The Museum Island

The world-renowned Museum Island (Museumsinsel) comprises five of Berlin's most famous museums and is an absolute must for any visitor to Berlin, if only to stroll around and take in the lovely buildings and waterside atmosphere. Friedrich Wilhelm III commissioned the Royal Museum (now the Altes Museum) in 1830, but the plan for an island of museums – intended as the embodiment of Enlightenment ideas about culture – came to fruition under Friedrich Wilhelm IV of Prussia. The site was further developed under successive Prussian kings. The range of artwork and architecture is startling, spanning two thousand years and featuring such treasures as the Roman gate of Miletus and the bust of Nefertiti as well as a dizzying range of paintings and sculptures. Though badly damaged during World War II, with the collections divided during the Cold War, sensitive renovations have seen the buildings revived. A visitor centre, the James-Simon-Galerie, opened in 2019 between the Neues Museum and Kupfergraben.

Berliner Dom (Cathedral)

MAP PAGE 42, POCKET MAP D13
Am Lustgarten 1 ⓦ berlinerdom.de.
Charge.

Berliner Dom

Designed by Julius Raschdorff in **Baroque** style with Italian Renaissance influences, Berlin's Protestant cathedral was intended as

Lustgarten

a counterpart to **St Peter's Basilica in Rome**. The present structure dates from 1905, but stands on the site of several earlier buildings, including the St Erasmus Chapel and a Neoclassical design by Schinkel dating from 1822. Restoration of the current interior began in 1984 and in 1993 the church reopened. It's a handsome and interesting building to explore, with notable eye candy including Sauer's organ, stained-glass windows designed by Anton von Werner and a marvellous dome intricately decorated with mosaics. You can get an excellent close-up view of the dome – and the entire interior – by climbing the 270 steps to the gallery. The most historically significant feature of the cathedral is its crypt, which holds more than eighty sarcophagi of Prussian royals, including those of Friedrich I and his queen, Sophie Charlotte.

Museum Island practicalities

The **website** for all Museum Island details is: ⓦ smb.museum. The nearest **stations** for the museums are Ⓢ Hackescher Markt and ⓤ Museumsinsel.

Three-day tickets for all state museums (including those in the Kulturforum, see page 64) and a wealth of private museums can be purchased online or in-person at most museum entrances, though these do not include special exhibitions. Note that entrance is always free for anyone under 18.

The **Berlin Welcome Card Museum Island** includes admission to many museums including the Museum Island, travel for up to 72 hours and up to 50 percent discount on many top attractions in Berlin. See ⓦ www.visitberlin.de.

In Berlin, the first Sunday of each month is **Museum Sunday**, when most museums (including those on Museum Island) have free admission. Free day tickets are available from the museum ticket offices. Expect to queue.

Neues Museum

Island landscape. It's difficult to believe that this charming rectangular park, a great spot for picnics or taking a pause between museum visits, has been used variously as a **military parade ground** (for Wilhelm I and Napoleon), mass protests (a huge anti-Nazi demo here in 1933 prompted the banning of demonstrations) and rallies (Hitler addressed up to a million people here). Bombed in the War and renamed Marx-Engels-Platz by the GDR, its current incarnation harks back to Peter Joseph Lenné's early nineteenth-century design with a central 13m-high fountain, as re-envisioned by German landscape architect Hans Loidl.

Lustgarten

MAP PAGE 42, POCKET MAP D13
Berlin's "Pleasure Garden" is a fundamental part of the Museum

Altes Museum

MAP PAGE 42, POCKET MAP D13
Am Lustgarten. Ⓦ smb.museum/en/museums-institutions/altes-museum. Charge.

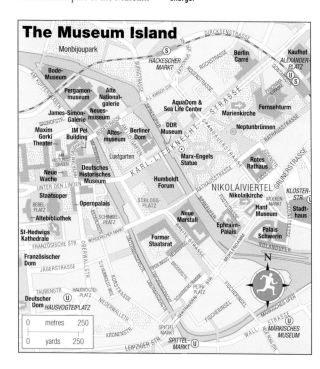

The Museum Island

DIRCKSENSTRASSE

Monbijoupark

Bode-Museum

Pergamon-museum

Alte National-galerie

James-Simon-Galerie

Neues-museum

Maxim Gorki Theater

IM Pei Building

Altes-museum

Berliner Dom

Lustgarten

Deutsches Historisches Museum

Neue Wache

Staatsoper

Opernpalais

Altebibliothek

St-Hedwigs Kathedrale

Französischer Dom

Deutscher Dom HAUSVOGTEIPLATZ

HACKESCHER MARKT

Berlin Carré

Kaufhof ALEXANDER-PLATZ

AquaDom & Sea Life Center

DDR Museum

Marienkirche

Fernsehturm

Neptunbrünnen

KARL-LIEBKNECHT-STR.

Marx-Engels Statue

Humboldt Forum

SCHLOSS-PLATZ

Neue Marstall

Former Staatsrat

Ephraim-Palais

Rotes Rathaus

NIKOLAIVIERTEL

Nikolaikirche

Hanf Museum

Palais Schwerin

KLOSTER-STR.

Stadt-haus

ROLANDUFER

N

MÄRKISCHES MUSEUM

SPITTEL-MARKT

| 0 | metres | 250 |
| 0 | yards | 250 |

Pergamonmuseum

The Altes Museum, built between 1823 and 1830 after a design by Karl Friedrich Schinkel, is **Berlin's oldest museum**. It's also one of the city's most important Classicist statements and a marvellous piece of architecture, all fluted Ionic columns, a beautiful rotunda filled with sculptures of Greek gods and a grand staircase that more than nods to Athens and Rome. As well as Greek statues downstairs, the upper floor contains a colossal range of Roman and Etruscan art – urns, shields, sarcophagi, friezes – all chronologically and thematically arranged.

Neues Museum

MAP PAGE 42, POCKET MAP D13
Bodestr. 1–3. Ⓦ neues-museum.de. Charge.
One of Museum Island's undoubted highlights, the misleadingly named Neues Museum was opened in 1859 to cater for the overspill of the by-then overcrowded Altes Museum. Largely destroyed during World War II, it was only reopened in 2009, fully restored by British architect David Chipperfield, whose distinguished makeover

has melded the old with the new, maintaining traces of war damage. Over three floors you'll find no less than twenty exhibition halls, each impressively designed and connected via a stunning winding staircase. As well as the archeological collections of the **Egyptian museum** and papyrus collection, there's plenty of pre- and early history, as well as works from classical antiquity. The big draw is the bust of Egyptian Queen Nefertiti – famously described as "the world's most beautiful woman" – but you could happily spend an entire day absorbing the endless exhibits.

Pergamonmuseum

MAP PAGE 42, POCKET MAP D12
Bodestr. 1–3. Ⓦ smb.museum/en/museums-institutions/pergamonmuseum. Closed at time of writing. Charge.
The Pergamonmuseum was built by Alfred Mussel in 1930 to house the artefacts from the nineteenth-century excavations of German archeologists in Pergamon and Asia Minor, perhaps most famously the controversial **"Priam's treasure"** – a cache of gold and other artefacts

discovered by classical archeologist Heinrich Schliemann, but whose authenticity and relationship to Homeric king Priam has long been in doubt. Essentially three museums in one, the museum offers a collection of Classical antiquities (part of which is also on display in the Altes Museum); the museum of the **Ancient Near East**; and the museum of **Islamic Art**. As with the Neues Museum, you can spend a day here easily, seeing highlights such as the **Pergamon Altar** from the second century BC and the Gallery of Hellenistic Art. Depending on what's on display at the time, check out the facade of the throne hall of King Nebuchadnezzar, the Market Gate of Miletus (an important example of Roman architecture) or the bright blue, glazed-brick Ishtar Gate of Babylon from the sixth century BC instead. The museum is currently closed for renovations but *Pergamonmuseum: Das Panorama*, an exhibition featuring a selection of artefacts from Pergamon and a

unique panoramic painting of the city, remains open.

Alte Nationalgalerie

MAP PAGE 42, POCKET MAP D12
Bodestr. 1–3. Ⓦ smb.museum/ en/museums-institutions/alte-nationalgalerie. Charge.

The Neoclassical Alte Nationalgalerie (Old National Gallery), designed to resemble a Greek temple, houses one of the country's most significant collections of nineteenth-century painting. Built between 1866 and 1876, the museum reopened in 2001 to showcase its wealth of Classical, Romantic, Impressionist and early Modernist masterpieces. Highlights include the Goethe-era landscapes, works by Jakob Philipp Hackert and Anton Graff and Romantic paintings by the likes of Caspar David Friedrich and Karl Friedrich Schinkel (a gifted landscape painter as well as one of Berlin's foremost architects). The Impressionist section, with its international "big hitters" **Manet**, **Monet**, **Renoir** and **Rodin**, is worth the visit alone.

Bode-Museum

MAP PAGE 42, POCKET MAP D12
Am Kupfergraben 1. Ⓦ smb.museum/en/museums-institutions/bode-museum. Charge.

The stately Bode-Museum, with its recognizable dome, was originally called the Kaiser Friedrich Museum, and was renamed in 1956 after its inaugural curator Wilhelm van Bode. Reopened following extensive refurbishments in 2006, the building is notable for its refined architectural details – the opulent staircases, monumental pilasters and demi-columns – as well as a wealth of art and artefacts from the **Byzantine** and **Medieval** periods. These are mainly from Germany but also come from major European art centres such as the Netherlands, Italy, France and Spain, and are culled from three

Bode-Museum

Alte Nationalgalerie

major state museum collections: the sculpture collection, with highlights including the terracotta statues from Luca della Robbia, the Madonna from Donatello and the sculptures of Desiderio da Settignano; the Museum of Byzantine Art – the only one of its kind in Germany; and the Numismatic Collection, a vast and impressive collection of coins (and other forms of currency) that range from the seventh century BC to the twenty-first century.

Humboldt Forum

MAP PAGE 42, POCKET MAP E13
Schloßpl. 1. ⓦ humboldtforum.org. Free with charge for special exhibitions.
The five museums to the north of the island got a new-old neighbour in 2020, with the opening of the Humboldt Forum in the rebuilt Berliner Schloss (Berlin Palace). The rebuilding of the palace was a contentious issue for years following reunification. The huge Hohenzollern palace was badly damaged during World War II and torn down by the GDR, replaced by the Palast der Republik and the Staatsratsgebäude. The former

was pulled down in turn following reunification, and discussions about what to do with the vast space ended with a decision to rebuild the old Baroque palace. Many locals and politicians weren't convinced by the plans. Should a notoriously debt-ridden city undertake such a costly, backwards-looking exercise? In 2007, the Bundestag (parliament) reached a compromise of sorts by deciding to rebuild the exterior facade with a modern interior and contemporary extension to the east, facing the Spree. They could do nothing to keep down the price, however, with the building becoming the most expensive cultural project in German history. The Forum brings together the collections of two former museums from Dahlem: the **Ethnologisches Museum** and the **Museum für Asiatische Kunst**. Billed as Germany's answer to the British Museum, the comparison holds true in terms of the museum's vast and rich collection of non-European artworks and artefacts, and its controversial showcasing of looted artworks.

Unter den Linden and the government quarter

Berlin's grand boulevard, named for the Linden (lime) trees that line it, runs east–west from the site of the former royal palace to the Brandenburg Gate. The road originated as a bridle path for Duke Friedrich Wilhelm in the seventeenth century; by the nineteenth century it was a popular gathering place for many Berliners and Unter den Linden was furnished with new buildings, including the Neoclassical Neue Wache. Despite appearances, most of the buildings are reconstructions. Nonetheless it maintains its upscale aura, reflected in the fine-dining restaurants and expensive shops that predominate. Beyond the Brandenburg Gate lies the modern, yet no less authoritative Regierungsviertel ("government quarter"), a cluster of buildings starting with the Reichstag that stretch along the Spree. A stroll along the river past the striking Paul Löbe Haus and the Bundeskanzleramt, towards the Hauptbahnhof, is a pleasant and architecturally interesting way to pass a couple of hours.

Deutsches Historisches Museum

MAP PAGE 48, POCKET MAP D13
Unter den Linden 2 Ⓤ/Ⓢ Friedrichstr.
Ⓦ dhm.de. The Zeughaus is closed at the time of writing. Charge.

The fascinating Deutsches Historisches Museum (German Historical Museum) is spread across two buildings: the unique Baroque Zeughaus (armoury) and a modern exhibition hall designed by Chinese-American architect I.M. Pei.

The **Zeughaus** was first used as a museum for German history during the years of the GDR (1952–90), essentially to espouse the Marxist-Leninist concept of history. In 2006 a permanent exhibition "German history in images and artefacts" was inaugurated in the three-hundred-year-old building (the oldest on Unter den Linden), which showcases two thousand years of

German history via eight thousand objects from the museum's extensive collections. Supplementing this are special temporary exhibitions displayed on the four floors of the spacious **Pei building**, with its glass-and-steel lobby and winding staircase. There's also a little-known **cinema**, entered from the Spree side of the museum, with a historically protected interior, and a refined **café** serving great breakfasts, lunches and cakes. The Zeughaus is currently closed for renovations, while the Pei building remains open.

Neue Wache

MAP PAGE 48, POCKET MAP D13
Unter den Linden 4 Ⓤ/Ⓢ Friedrichstr.
Ⓣ 030 25 00 2333. Free.

The Neue Wache (New Guard House) was Karl Friedrich Schinkel's first major commission in Berlin – he rose to the occasion by building a leading example of German Neoclassicism. Originally constructed as a **guardhouse** for the troops of the crown prince of Prussia, the building became a memorial to the Wars of Liberation (Napoleonic Wars) until 1918. From 1931 onwards it was a memorial for World War I, and the inner courtyard was covered over, apart from a small opening in the roof letting through a slither of symbolic light. Post World War II, the GDR leadership turned it into a monument for the victims of fascism and militarism. An eternal flame was placed in a cube above the ashes of an unknown concentration camp prisoner and an unknown fallen soldier. After German reunification, the GDR memorial piece was removed and replaced by an enlarged version of Käthe Kollwitz's sculpture *Mother with her Dead Son* (*Pietà*). This sculpture is directly under the oculus, its exposure to the elements a metaphor for the suffering of civilians during World War II.

Bebelplatz

MAP PAGE 48, POCKET MAP C13
Ⓤ Französische Str.

This historical square on the south side of Unter den Linden was constructed between 1741 and 1743 and was originally known as Opernplatz. Though framed by the opulent **Staatsoper** (see page 55), a library and the swanky *Hotel de Rome* (see page 145), it remains best known for the 1933 Nazi book burning that took place here, as instigated by propaganda minister Joseph Goebbels. The Nazis burned some twenty thousand books, including works by Thomas Mann, Erich Maria Remarque, Heinrich Heine and Karl Marx. At the centre of the square is a **memorial** of the burning by Micha Ullman, which consists of a glass-covered view into an underground chamber of empty bookshelves. Nearby, an engraving of a line from Heinrich Heine translates as: "Where they burn books, they ultimately burn people".

DB Palais Populaire

MAP PAGE 48, POCKET MAP C13
Unter den Linden 5 Ⓢ Französisches Str.
Ⓦ www.db-palaispopulaire.de. Charge.
Located in the 18th century Prinzessin Palais (the rooms were redesigned by Kuehn Malvezzi) – three times the size of the

Bebelplatz

Bebelplatz

former DB Kunsthalle – the Palais Populaire opened in mid 2018. It showcases all manner of things from local, global and future cultures and strives to be an "open house" – combining an innovative forum for visitors with art, culture and sports. The Palais Populaire's opening exhibition, "The World on Paper", showcased 300 works of contemporary art, the most comprehensive works from the DB collection. Besides art, the museum hosts lectures and other events.

Gendarmenmarkt

MAP PAGE 48, POCKET MAP C14
Ⓤ Hausvogteiplatz/Französische Str./ Stadtmitte.

The Gendarmenmarkt, one of Berlin's most beautiful squares, was created at the end of the seventeenth century as a market place (then called the Linden Markt), but its current name comes from the Regiment Gens d'Armes

that had their stables here from 1736 to 1773. Despite its inherent grandness, it's a surprisingly quiet place defined by three landmark buildings: the Französischer Dom, Deutscher Dom and the **Konzerthaus** (Concert Hall, see page 55), which frame a central statue of Friedrich Schiller. The **Französischer Dom** and **Deutscher Dom** are two seemingly identical churches facing each other across the square, poised in a standoff for visitor attention. The Französischer Dom (French Cathedral) is older, built between 1701 and 1705 by the Huguenot community, and contains a Huguenot museum, a restaurant on the top floor and a viewing platform. The pentagonal Deutscher Dom (German Cathedral), at the southern end of the square, was designed by Martin Grünberg, built in 1708 by Giovanni Simonetti and modified in 1785 after a design by Carl von Gontard, who added the

ACCOMMODATION
Adlon Kempinski	3
Arcotel John F	5
Arte Luise Kunsthotel	1
Hotel de Rome	4
Westin Grand	2

SHOPS
Ampelmann Shop	2
Dussmann das KulturKaufhaus	1
Galeries Lafayette	3
Mall of Berlin	5
Quartier 206	4

CLUBS & VENUES
Komische Oper Berlin	4
Konzerthaus Berlin	5
Maxim Gorki Theater	2
Staatsoper	3
Tausend	1

domed tower. A popular Christmas market is held on the square during the holidays.

Akademie der Künste

MAP PAGE 48, POCKET MAP B14
Pariser Platz 4 (and Hanseatenweg 10, Tiergarten) ◐/⑤ Brandenburger Tor
Ⓦ adk.de. Charge.
Founded as the Prussian Academy of Arts in 1696 by Friedrich III, this public corporation continues its original mission to support and foster the arts. Its prestigious members have included Goethe, Mendelssohn-Bartholdy and Brecht; Max Liebermann headed the institution in the 1920s after the academy introduced a literature section. Under Hitler it was used as a headquarters for architect Albert Speer to redesign Berlin into "Germania", before being bombed almost to the ground (only the exhibition halls remained intact). During the GDR era it was turned into studios for Academy members like the sculptor Fritz Cremer and several master scholars such as Wieland Förster and Werner Stötzer. The glass-facade building, designed by Günter Behnisch, lies directly in front of what's left of the original academy, and its current members include German Nobel laureate Günter Grass, architects Daniel Libeskind and Sir Norman Foster and composer Sir Harrison Birtwistle. The venue holds a number of **lectures**, **exhibits** and **workshops**.

Brandenburg Gate

MAP PAGE 48, POCKET MAP A13
Pariser Platz ◐/⑤ Brandenburger Tor.
A former city gate (the only remaining of the period), the Brandenburg Gate (Brandenburger Tor) is one of the most recognizable icons of Berlin, if not Europe. Commissioned by Friedrich Wilhelm II of Prussia as a sign of

CAFÉS & BARS	
Café Nö!	11
Einstein	4
Newton Bar	12
Windhorst	2

RESTAURANTS	
Bocca di Bacco	7
Borchardt	9
Charlotte & Fritz	8
Cookies Cream	5
Crackers	6
Ishin	3
Käfer Dachgarten	1
Lutter & Wegner	10

Unter den Linden and the government quarter

Brandenburg Gate

pop into the Room of Silence on the north side, built specifically for visitors to rest and reflect.

Memorial to the Murdered Jews of Europe

MAP PAGE 48, POCKET MAP A14
Cora-Berliner-Str. 1 ⓤ/Ⓢ **Brandenburger Tor** ⓦ holocaust-mahnmal.de. Free.

Peter Eisenman's hugely controversial 2711 sombre concrete slabs (stelae) are arranged in a neat grid spread across 19,000 square metres of land near the Brandenburg Gate, the memorial's grand scale intended as a reminder of the magnitude of the Holocaust. The slabs are purposefully varying in height to give visitors walking among them a sense of disorientation and confusion, though from above the slabs appear to make a wave-like form. Soon after construction began in 2003, a Swiss newspaper reported that a subsidiary of the company hired to produce the anti-graffiti substance to cover the stelae, Degussa, had created the poison gas used to exterminate so many in the Nazi death camps of the Holocaust. Rather than spend an additional €2 million to undo the work and hire another company, work continued.

As powerful as the memorial is, it's the 800-square-metre underground **information centre** (located in the southeastern corner) that really leaves you reeling. The centre holds factual exhibits to balance the abstract memorial above, including personal information about many of the victims and a video archive ("Voices of Survival") where you can listen to Holocaust survivor testimonies in many languages, or even search for specific places, people or events in the database.

peace, and built by Carl Gotthard Langhans in 1788 from a design based upon the Propylaea (the gateway to the Acropolis in Athens), the gate has at various times been a symbol of victory, peace, division and unity. After the 1806 Prussian defeat at the Battle of Jena-Auerstedt, Napoleon took the Quadriga (added in 1793 by Johann Gottfried Schadow) to Paris. After Napoleon's defeat in 1814 and the Prussian occupation of Paris by General Ernst von Pfuel, the Quadriga was restored to Berlin. The Gate survived World War II and was one of the damaged structures still standing in the ruins of Pariser Platz in 1945. In December 2000, the Brandenburg Gate was closed for a €4 million private refurbishment by the Stiftung Denkmalschutz Berlin (Berlin Monument Conservation Foundation), reopening less than two years later. Today, it still draws punters by the busload. The best way to enjoy it is to stroll towards it via **Unter den Linden**, taking in the trees and run of shops, glamorous theatres and excellent museums along the way. It's a very touristy spot, so for a bit of peace and quiet

The Reichstag

MAP PAGE 48, POCKET MAP A13
Platz der Republik 1 ⓤ **Bundestag** ⓦ bundestag.de. Roof terrace and dome accessible on prearranged guided tours or with a restaurant reservation. Charge.

The Reichstag, the seat of the German Parliament, has played a crucial role in several of the city's most significant historic events. After the founding of the German Empire in 1872, German architect Paul Wallot was commissioned to create this imposing neo-Renaissance parliament building. It was constructed between 1884 and 1894, mainly funded with wartime reparation money from France – following Prussia's defeat of France in 1871. The famous inscription "Dem Deutschen Volke" (To the German People) was added in 1916 by Wilhelm II. In 1933 a fire destroyed much of the Reichstag. Though it remains uncertain how the fire started, the Communists were blamed, allowing Hitler and the Nazis to consolidate their power, suspend civil liberties and turn Germany into a dictatorship. The building was further damaged at the end of the War, when the Soviets entered Berlin. The picture of a Red Army soldier raising the Soviet flag on the Reichstag is one of the most famous twentieth-century images and symbolized Germany's defeat. The Reichstag was rebuilt between 1958 and 1972, but the central dome and most of the ornamentation were removed. During Berlin's division the West German parliament assembled here once a year as a way to indicate that Bonn was only a temporary capital – and indeed, after reunification, the Bundestag relocated here. The building was renovated again from 1995 to 1999, when the glass dome designed by Sir Norman Foster was added. At first the subject of much controversy, the dome has become one of the city's most recognized landmarks. Since April 1999, the Reichstag is once again the seat of the Bundestag – and also one of the city's largest attractions. Not all of the building is open to the public: the most popular (and accessible) part is the glass dome, which features a roof terrace, **restaurant** and fantastic views over the city. It's currently only open to visitors with a **restaurant reservation**, who have registered to attend a sitting or lecture, or who sign up in advance for a guided tour. The audioguides (free) last twenty minutes.

St Hedwig's Cathedral

MAP PAGE 48, POCKET MAP D14
Hinter der Katholischen Kirche 3
Ⓤ Französische Str. Ⓦ hedwigs-kathedrale.de. Guided tours available on request. Free.
The seat of the archbishop of Berlin, St Hedwig's Cathedral was the first Catholic church to be built in Germany after the Protestant Reformation. Consecrated in 1773, it was completely destroyed by Allied bombs in 1943, but reconstruction began in 1952 and was finally completed in 1963. The exterior is striking, but it's also worth popping inside to see the interior of the dome, composed of 84 reinforced concrete segments, and the impressive **hanging organ** (built in 1978 to replace one destroyed in the War), made by Klais of Bonn. St Hedwig's closed to visitors in 2018 as it underwent extensive renovations. It is set to reopen in time for Christmas 2024 with a modern, minimalist interior.

Museum der Dinge

MAP PAGE 48, POCKET MAP D14
Leipziger Str. 54 Ⓤ Spittelmarkt
Ⓦ museumderdinge.de. Charge.
A museum dedicated to the somewhat ambiguous culture of "things" could have gone either way. It succeeds by presenting an interesting array of implements – around 25,000 to be precise. Everyday houseware, furniture and knick-knacks are mixed with the unusual, spanning the nineteenth century to the present day. One of the chief attractions is the modular **"Frankfurt Kitchen"** designed by Viennese architect Margarete Schütte-Lihotzky in 1926 – the original model for the fitted kitchen of today.

Shops

Ampelmann Shop

MAP PAGE 48, POCKET MAP C13
Unter den Linden 35 ⓤ Französische Str./ Ⓢ Friedrichstr. ⓦ ampelmann.de.

The very first traffic lights to feature Karl Peglau's red and green Ampelmännchen stood on Unter den Linden. Fitting then, that this flagship store is here to pay tribute in the shape of thirty sets of traffic lights from all over the world, and a wealth of related gifts and souvenirs. There's also a small café selling coffee and snacks.

Dussmann das KulturKaufhaus

MAP PAGE 48, POCKET MAP C13
Friedrichstr. 90 ⓤ/Ⓢ Friedrichstr. ⓦ kulturkaufhaus.de.

This giant store has five levels of books, CDs, vinyl and DVDs – and a large section of books in English and ten other foreign languages across two floors.

Galeries Lafayette

MAP PAGE 48, POCKET MAP C14
Friedrichstr. 76–78 ⓤ Stadtmitte ⓦ galerieslafayette.de.

This elegant branch of the Parisian store opened in 1996. Housed in a glass temple designed by Jean Nouvel, it stocks every super-exclusive brand you can think of, from Agent Provocateur to Yves Saint Laurent. There's also a vast variety of gourmet foods.

Mall of Berlin

MAP PAGE 48, POCKET MAP B15
Leipziger Platz 12 Ⓢ Potsdamer Platz ⓦ mallofberlin.de.

Housed on the site of the city's former Wertheim Department Store (an architectural and retail highlight during the Weimar era), this is Germany's biggest shopping centre. Housing 270 stores, apartments and a hotel, it's a modern, elegant space with a mix of high-street names (Zara, H&M), independent fashion boutiques and luxury outlets (Hugo Boss, Ralph

Galeries Lafayette

Lauren). There's a second-floor food court.

Quartier 206

MAP PAGE 48, POCKET MAP C14
Friedrichstr. 71 ⓤ Stadtmitte
ⓦ quartier206berlin.de.
Unapologetically posh department store, all set in a lavish, Art Deco-inspired interior.

Restaurants

Bocca di Bacco

MAP PAGE 48, POCKET MAP C14
Friedrichstr. 167–168 ⓤ Französische Str.
ⓦ boccadibacco.de.
Bocca di Bacco blends a down-to-earth atmosphere with high-quality cuisine, inspired by Tuscany and other parts of Italy. The menu includes pasta, game, fish and plenty of wonderful desserts. The three-course lunch is a pretty good deal. €€€

Borchardt

MAP PAGE 48, POCKET MAP C14
Französische Str. 47 ⓤ Französische Str.
ⓦ borchardt-restaurant.de.
A reincarnation of a nineteenth-century meeting place for high society, *Borchardt* mark two is a tasteful facsimile with marble columns, plush seating and an Art Nouveau mosaic that was discovered during renovations. The place draws politicians, celebrities and tourists, and cuisine is high-quality French-German – though if you're not a regular, service is likely to be offhand at best. €€€€

Charlotte & Fritz

MAP PAGE 48, POCKET MAP C14
Regent Berlin, Charlottenstr. 49
ⓤ Französische Str. ⓦ charlotteundfritz.com.
Charlotte & Fritz (formerly *Fischers Fritz*) is headed by Jörg Lawerenz, who has created a menu based on regional cuisine specialities, while focusing on fine meats. At lunchtime, it also offers weekly changing business lunches. €€€€

Cookies Cream

MAP PAGE 48, POCKET MAP C13
Behrenstr. 55 ⓤ Französische Str.
ⓦ cookiescream.de.
Deliberately difficult to find (it's behind the *Westin Grand* on Friedrichstr.; see website for creative directions) this stylish restaurant is worth seeking out. It's one of the best vegetarian restaurants in the city, with a Michelin star (first gained in 2018) to prove it. It's pricey but not prohibitive if you're looking for a treat. The seasonal, inventive food is worth it. €€€€

Crackers

MAP PAGE 48, POCKET MAP C13
Friedrichstr. 158 ⓤ Französische Str.
ⓦ crackersberlin.com.
Downstairs from *Cookies Cream* (see above), the equally chic *Crackers* offers a European-nouveau menu of meat and fish (and some vegetarian options), a great cocktail bar and hip service. DJ dinner sets on Fri & Sat. €€€€

Borchardt

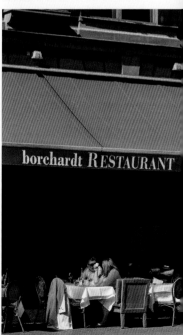

Einstein

Ishin

MAP PAGE 48, POCKET MAP C13 Mittelstr. 24 ⓊＳ Brandenburger Tor/ Friedrichstr. Ⓦ ishin.de.

There are two *Ishin* restaurants in Berlin. The interior of this central one is slightly functional but the decent, fresh sushi, good prices and quick service make it very popular, especially for lunch. There's a happy hour all day Wednesday and Saturday (plus Mon, Tues, Thurs & Fri till 4pm), plenty of veggie dishes and free green tea. €€€

Käfer Dachgarten

MAP PAGE 48, POCKET MAP A13 Platz der Republik 1 Ⓤ Bundestag Ⓦ feinkost-kaefer.de/berlin.

Famous for its location on the roof of the Reichstag and its 180-degree view of eastern Berlin, this restaurant specializes in gourmet renditions of regional German dishes. A reservation here also means you get to avoid the registration process through the Bundestag. €€€€

Lutter & Wegner

MAP PAGE 48, POCKET MAP C14 Charlottenstr. 56 Ⓤ Französische Str. Ⓦ l-w-berlin.de.

This refined, airy Austro-German restaurant is the finest of the *Lutter & Wagner* mini empire – it was here the wine merchant started (in 1811). Prices are high, but that's what happens when *The New York Times* crowns your Wiener Schnitzel the best outside Vienna (though the Sauerbraten is the real highlight). €€€€€

Cafés and bars

Café Nö!

MAP PAGE 48, POCKET MAP B14 Glinkastr. 23 Ⓤ Französische Str. Ⓦ cafe-noe.de.

This popular wine bar-restaurant serves good food for good prices and has a great atmosphere when the evening swings around. The menu includes *Flammkuchen,* truffle pasta and the like, plus lunch deals. €€€

Einstein

MAP PAGE 48, POCKET MAP B13

Unter den Linden 42 Ⓤ/Ⓢ Brandenburger Tor Ⓦ einstein-udl.de.

The younger sibling to the famous *Café Einstein* (see page 134), this branch doesn't have the same panache, but it's popular with Berlin's cultural elite and serves excellent Austro-Hungarian specialities. Also good for a coffee and cake. €

Newton Bar

MAP PAGE 48, POCKET MAP C14

Charlottenstr. 57 Ⓤ Stadtmitte Ⓦ newton-bar.de.

Dedicated to photographer Helmut Newton, this classy bar, all leather chairs and oak furnishings, is popular with a mature, well-heeled crowd. The large windows look out onto Gendarmenmarkt, though since a huge Newton photograph called *Big Nudes* covers one wall, you won't be short of things to look at either way. The cocktail are expertly poured.

Windhorst

MAP PAGE 48, POCKET MAP C13

Dorotheenstr. 65 Ⓤ/Ⓢ Friedrichstr. Ⓦ windhorst-bar.de.

Though it's not in a residential area, this tucked-away cocktail haven feels like a neighbourhood spot. It's a smart, fairly simple place, but the cocktails are above average and go well with the jazz (on vinyl) that they love to play.

Clubs and venues

Komische Oper Berlin

MAP PAGE 48, POCKET MAP C13

Behrenstr. 55–57 Ⓤ Französische Str. Ⓦ komische-oper-berlin.de.

Presenting everything from opera and German operetta to musicals and baroque, the Comic Opera – the smallest of Berlin's three opera houses – was built between 1891 and 1892. Since 2004 it has been operated by the Berliner Opernstiftung.

Konzerthaus Berlin

MAP PAGE 48, POCKET MAP C14

Gendarmenmarkt Ⓤ Französische Str. Ⓦ konzerthaus.de.

The concert house was built on the ruins of the national theatre by Schinkel in 1821. Since 1984 it has been the home of the Konzerthausorchester Berlin and is numbered amongst the best classical concert venues in the world. German-language tours are available (Sat 1pm; 75min, charge).

Maxim Gorki Theater

MAP PAGE 48, POCKET MAP D13

Am Festungsgraben 2 Ⓤ/Ⓢ Friedrichstr. Ⓦ gorki.de.

Named after the Russian socialist-realist author, this large theatre hosts classic dramas by him plus contemporary works by the likes of Fassbinder. All shows except premieres have English surtitles.

Staatsoper

MAP PAGE 48, POCKET MAP D13

Unter den Linden 7 Ⓤ Unter den Linden Ⓦ staatsoper-berlin.de.

This is one of the world's leading opera houses, its history going back to the eighteenth century and including illustrious conductors like Richard Strauss.

Tausend

MAP PAGE 48, POCKET MAP B12

Schiffbauerdamm 11 Ⓤ/Ⓢ Friedrichstr. Ⓦ tausendberlin.com.

Decorated with an enormous eye that emits a golden glow over the tunnel-shaped space, this upmarket bar-club, quite anonymous from the outside, attracts a dapper crowd, so it's advisable to turn up looking the part. Inside you'll find a mix of upbeat disco, jazz and R&B. At the back of the club you'll find a hidden, high-end Ibero-Asian fusion restaurant, *Cantina*, by chef Octavio Osés Bravo. Reservations essential.

Alexanderplatz and the Nikolaiviertel

Beautifully bleak or just plain bleak, Alexanderplatz – or Alex, as it's colloquially known – is one of Berlin's best-known squares. Named in honour of a visit from Russian Tsar Alexander I in 1805, by the start of the twentieth century it had become a commercial centre busy enough to rival Potsdamer Platz. Under the GDR it was a nondescript pedestrianized area and in 1989 was the site of the Peaceful Revolution, the largest demonstration in the history of East Germany. Today its grey, concrete GDR tower blocks, themselves towered over by the needle-like spire of the Fernsehturm (TV Tower), join more recent buildings like the Alexa shopping mall and the Saturn electronics store to create a grandly proportioned, strikingly austere commercial and transport hub. More conventionally scenic, though touristy, is the adjacent Nikolaiviertel, with its pretty old-town feel and various museums, a reconstruction of the historical heart of the city that dates back to the thirteenth century.

Berliner Fernsehturm

MAP PAGE 58, POCKET MAP F12
Panoramastr. 1a ⓤ/Ⓢ Alexanderplatz

Ⓦ tv-turm.de. Charge.
The city's most visible structure, the 368m concrete spike known as the

Berliner Fernsehturm

Fernsehturm (television tower), is the building most likely to crop up in all your photographs when you get home – whether you realized you'd been photographing it or not. Built in 1969 as a broadcasting system for East Berlin, and intended as a showpiece structure for the **GDR**, visible in West Berlin, it has a visitor platform at 203m – a **lift** zooms you up in forty seconds – and two **VR experiences**, detailing the building of the tower and covering nine centuries of Berlin's history. Above the visitor platform, there's also a **rotating restaurant**, *Sphere*, that serves coffee, snacks and meals while revolving once around the tower's axis every sixty minutes. The tower receives around a million visitors a year and the queues can be long whatever the weather. You don't need a reservation for the tower, but it can be handy for the restaurant (in high season). Another option is to book a fast-track ticket on the website in advance, which enables you to dodge the queues and has an option for a table reservation.

If the sun's out when you're out and about, take a look up at the Fernsehturm and see if you can spot the cross that's reflected across the main steel sphere: the religious symbolism caused a great deal of embarrassment for the atheist GDR government.

DDR Museum

DDR Museum

MAP PAGE 58, POCKET MAP E13
Karl-Liebknecht-Str. 1 Ⓤ/
Ⓢ **Alexanderplatz** Ⓦ **ddr-museum.de.**
Charge.
Located opposite the Berliner Dom (see page 40), this collection of memorabilia from the Deutsche Demokratische Republik (DDR/GDR) makes for a fun, interactive and informative visit. There are screens to touch, buttons to press, drawers to open – even a Trabant to sit in and a bugged apartment to listen in on.

Divided into three differently themed areas ("Public Life", "State and Ideology", "Life in a Tower Block"), visitors get to inspect a reconstruction of a GDR living room, experience what it's like to have your phone bugged and ponder the East German penchant for public nudity – little wonder it's one of the most visited museums in Berlin.

Though many of the displays feed on the current trend for *Ostalgie*, there is also an emphasis on the darker side of GDR life – Party, State, prison – making this a more rounded experience than it may first appear.

Rotes Rathaus

MAP PAGE 58, POCKET MAP E13
Rathausstr. 15 Ⓤ/
Ⓢ **Alexanderplatz** Ⓣ **030 90 260. Free.**
This distinctive building gets its name (which means "red town hall") from the red clinker brick of its facade. The building, inspired by Italian High Renaissance architecture, was erected in the 1860s. During communist times,

it was East Berlin's town hall, when the red in the name really came into its own; today it's the office of the city mayor and is the political centre of power in Greater Berlin. Its neo-Renaissance clock tower and frieze depicting Berlin's history until 1879 in 36 terracotta plaques, each 6m long, are its most impressive architectural features. At the top of the grand stairwell is a coat-of-arms hall and some exhibits. The building also has a **cafeteria** with low-price lunches.

Marienkirche

MAP PAGE 58, POCKET MAP E12
Karl-Liebknecht-Str. 8 ⓤ /
Ⓢ **Alexanderplatz** Ⓦ **marienkirche-berlin. de. Free.**

Standing somewhat incongruously at the edge of Alexanderplatz and the Marx-Engels-Forum, the Marienkirche (church of St Mary) – one of **Berlin's oldest churches** – is the last remnant of its time in the area. Built some time in the thirteenth century, its oldest part is the granite base, upon which a hall church (Hallenkirche) stands. The tower was added during the fifteenth century, and the steeple in 1790 by Carl Gotthard Langhan, architect of the Brandenburg Gate. The church escaped heavy damage during World War II and was later fully restored. Visitors today can see *The Dance of Death* (*Totentanz*), a large fresco (2m high, 22m long), dating from about 1485, that was discovered in 1860 under layers of paint and depicts various classes of society dancing with Death. Other notable artworks include a bronze baptismal font from 1437, *The Crucifixion,* painted by Michael Ribestein in 1562 and an alabaster pulpit created by Andreas Schlüter in 1703, decorated with reliefs of John the Baptist and personifications of Faith, Hope and Love.

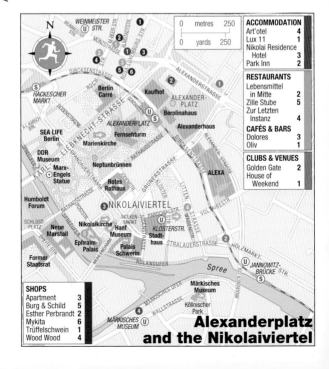

Alexanderplatz and the Nikolaiviertel

ACCOMMODATION
Art'otel	4
Lux 11	1
Nikolai Residence Hotel	3
Park Inn	2

RESTAURANTS
Lebensmittel in Mitte	2
Zille Stube	5
Zur Letzten Instanz	4

CAFÉS & BARS
Dolores	3
Oliv	1

CLUBS & VENUES
Golden Gate	2
House of Weekend	1

SHOPS
Apartment	3
Burg & Schild	5
Esther Perbrandt	2
Mykita	6
Trüffelschwein	1
Wood Wood	4

Ephraim-Palais

SEA LIFE Berlin

MAP PAGE 58, POCKET MAP E13
Spandauer Str. 3 ⑤ Hackescher Markt
Ⓦ visitsealife.com. Charge.

Sadly diminished since its chief claim to fame, the AquaDom – the world's largest cylindrical fish aquarium, a 25m-tall acrylic glass aquarium, with built-in transparent elevator – ruptured, causing a huge amount of damage to nearby facilities and killing the majority of the 1,500 fish contained within. The main aquarium is still intact, insightful enough and a well-laid-out exhibition, though it lacks the comprehensive scope and diversity – not to mention the manatees and sharks – of the Zoo Aquarium (see page 120).

Ephraim Palais

MAP PAGE 58, POCKET MAP E13
Poststr. 16 Ⓤ Klosterstr. Ⓦ stadtmuseum.de/en/museum/museum-ephraim-palais. Charge.

This attractive **Rococo-style** residential palace, located in the southern corner of Berlin's Nikolaiviertel, is a replica of a 1762 original built by Veitel Heine Ephraim, a court jeweller. His original building was torn down in 1935–36 when the Mühlendamm was widened, but a painstaking reconstruction has produced an exquisite place, with its elegantly curving, decorated facade (complete with cherubs), Tuscan columns, wrought-iron balconies and an oval staircase and ornate ceiling crafted by Schlüter. The building is today home to a museum of Berlin's history and culture – the permanent **"BerlinZEIT"** exhibition is well worth a look.

Märkisches Museum

MAP PAGE 58, POCKET MAP F14
Am Köllnischen Park 5 Ⓤ /
⑤ Jannowitzbrücke Closed at time of writing for extensive renovations.
Ⓦ stadtmuseum.de/en/museum/maerkisches-museum. Charge.

The red-brick Märkisches Museum, built at the turn of the twentieth century, is the

Hanf Museum

headquarters of Berlin's City Museum Foundation. The permanent exhibition "Here is Berlin" invites you to stroll through the city's streets and discover how Berlin has changed over the centuries. The museum also hosts a wide array of **art-historic collections** in its atmospheric rooms, with medieval sculptures, artefacts and paintings telling the story of Berlin from the first settlers until now (German text only). Thoughtfully divided into sections of the city – Unter den Linden, Friedrichstrasse and so on – favourites include a working mechanical musical instrument that's shown off every Sunday (3pm), seven original graffitied segments of the Berlin Wall and a Kaiserpanorama: a stereoscope dating from around 1900 that produces a fascinating 3D show of images from nineteenth-century Berlin. The museum closed to the public in 2023, set to reopen in 2028 following extensive renovations.

Hanf Museum

MAP PAGE 58, POCKET MAP E13
Mühlendamm 5 Ⓤ Klosterstr.
Ⓦ hanfmuseum.de. Charge.
Opened in 1994, the Hanf Museum is one of the only museums in Germany devoted exclusively to the agricultural, manufacturing, industrial and legal aspects of **hemp** – a plant most commonly associated with marijuana. This museum, while slightly dingy, isn't just for the stoners: the aim is to give a broader overview of this fascinating botanical treasure and its myriad applications, from textile and paper to medicine and cosmetics. There's also a pleasant **café** where you can try hemp tea and coffee with a side of hemp cake.

Shops

Apartment

MAP PAGE 58, POCKET MAP F12
Memhardstr. 8 ⓤ/Ⓢ Alexanderplatz
Ⓦ apartmentberlin.de.
You'll have to be careful not to
walk right past what looks like
an all-white art space: the goods
lie downstairs (follow the spiral
staircase), where you'll find jeans,
jackets, shoes and accessories with a
distinctly Berlin twist.

Burg & Schild

MAP PAGE 58, POCKET MAP E12
Rosa-Luxemburg-Str. 3 ⓤ Rosa-
Luxemburg-Platz Ⓦ burgundschild.com.
Visit a long-vanished America by
way of brands like Iron Heart,
Indigofera, Filson and Buzz
Rickson's, all on display alongside
vintage motorbikes that generate an
authentic odour of oil and tar.

Esther Perbandt

MAP PAGE 58, POCKET MAP E12
Almstadtstr. 3 ⓤ Weinmeisterstr.
Ⓦ estherperbandt.com.
A relative veteran of the Berlin
fashion scene, Esther Perbandt sells
(pricey) rock-adjacent and avant-
garde styles with an androgynous
slant. As well as clothing, expect
bags, belts and jewellery.

Mykita

MAP PAGE 58, POCKET MAP F12
Rosa-Luxemburg-Str. 6 ⓤ/
Ⓢ Alexanderplatz Ⓦ mykita.com.
Sunglasses and spectacles with a
stylish twist, sold in a hip, minimal
space with large street-facing
windows. Berlin-based Mykita
opened in 2003 and has since
achieved international prominence.

Trüffelschwein

MAP PAGE 58, POCKET MAP F11
Rosa-Luxemburg-Str. 21 ⓤ Rosa-
Luxemburg-Platz Ⓦ trueffelschweinberlin.
com.
This pleasant, airy store sells
everything menswear, from smart

Burg & Schild

shoes and trendy jumpers to belts
and dapper swimwear. Labels
include Hannes Roether, Howlin'
and La Paz.

Wood Wood

MAP PAGE 58, POCKET MAP F12
Rochstr. 3–4 ⓤ/Ⓢ Alexanderplatz
Ⓦ woodwood.com.
One of the best stops in the area
for all things streetwear, this
long-serving Berlin branch of
Copenhagen-based Wood Wood
stocks an incredible sneaker
collection plus contemporary
fashion items.

Restaurants

Lebensmittel in Mitte

MAP PAGE 58, POCKET MAP E12
Rochstr. 2 ⓤ Weinmeisterstr. ⓣ 030 27
59 61 30.
If you're a fan of "slow" home
cooking, this unassuming spot
on Rochstrasse is a good choice.
Specializing in German cuisine
(mainly from the south), the menu
features hearty soups, sausages,
sauerkraut and *Spätzle* (a type of
soft egg noodle), as well as a decent

selection of German/Austrian wines and Bavarian beer, all served against a homely, elegant backdrop. €€€

Zille Stube

MAP PAGE 58, POCKET MAP E13
Spreeufer 3 Ⓤ Klosterstr. Ⓦ zillestube-nikolaiviertel.de.

A great place to break up a stroll around the Nikolaiviertel, the menu here features Berlin specialities like *Currywurst* and *Eisbein* (knuckle of pork), all served in cosy, time-warp surroundings. Named after the area's most famous caricaturist, Heinrich Zille, there's an evening show every couple of months that transports guests back to the artist's turn-of-the-century Berlin. €€€

Zur Letzten Instanz

MAP PAGE 58, POCKET MAP F13
Waisenstr. 14–16 Ⓤ Klosterstr.
Ⓦ zurletzteninstanz.de.

Yes it's the oldest restaurant in Berlin (the building goes right back to 1561), yes the interior is textbook Alt Berlin and yes it's a tourist haunt, but the food here – traditional dishes like pork knuckle, dumplings and Berlin meatballs – is delicious and care is taken to source ingredients from local producers. Portions are hearty and there's Pilsner on draught to wash it all down. €€€

Cafés and bars

Dolores

MAP PAGE 58, POCKET MAP E12
Rosa-Luxemburg-Str. 7 Ⓤ /
Ⓢ Alexanderplatz Ⓦ dolores-online.de.

Run by Germans who spent a considerable time in California, Berlin's first burrito shop is a basic but colourful spot that offers pre-prepared "classics", "make-your-own", customizable burritos and also quesadillas, salads and soups. A good spot for a cheap, filling bite or takeaway, and they also have great vegan and vegetarian options. There is a second branch

Zur Letzten Instanz

Oliv

in Schöneberg (Bayreuther Str. 36
Ⓤ Wittenbergplatz). €

Oliv

MAP PAGE 58, POCKET MAP E12
Münzstr. 8 Ⓤ Weinmeisterstr./Rosa-
Luxemburg-Platz Ⓦ oliv-cafe.de.
With a modern interior, great
coffee and decent, unpretentious
food (sandwiches, quiches, soups,
cakes), *Oliv* is a pleasant spot
for breakfast or lunch, and very
conveniently located if you're
seeking respite from boutique
bashing. €€

Clubs and venues

Golden Gate

MAP PAGE 58, POCKET MAP J5
Dircksenstr. 77–78 Ⓤ/Ⓢ Jannowitzbrücke
Ⓦ goldengate-berlin.de.
Lurking beneath the tracks near
Jannowitzbrücke train station
(close to the river Spree), this club
consists of two wilfully shabby
rooms kitted out in secondhand
furniture and is dedicated to
two- or three-day-long free-for-
alls. The crowds here tend to be a
dressed-down, unpretentious lot
who arrive well after midnight to
try their luck with the difficult
bouncers. Music policy is mostly
house and techno but there are
sometimes surprises.

House of Weekend

MAP PAGE 58, POCKET MAP F12
Alexanderstr. 7 (15th floor and
open rooftop) Ⓤ/Ⓢ Alexanderplatz
Ⓦ weekendclub.berlin.
Accessed via a lift that shoots
punters up to the top of a
Communist-era tower block, this
chic, spacious club has attained
veteran status in the city thanks
to its consistently good house and
techno parties. International guests
and high-profile residents play most
weekends. The wonderful roof
terrace – open from 7pm daily in
summer – is a must.

Potsdamer Platz and Tiergarten

A major public transport hub and popular entertainment district, Potsdamer Platz was one of the liveliest squares in Europe during the 1920s. Reduced to rubble during the War, afterwards it became – literally – a no-man's land, sandwiched between the different sectors. What little remained was levelled when the Berlin Wall went up in 1961. After the Wall fell, it became the largest construction site in Europe as an ambitious rebuilding programme started. Commercial, even futuristic in tone, the centrepiece today is The Center Potsdamer Platz (formerly the Sony Center), surrounded by a new U-Bahn station and a few slabs from the old Berlin Wall. Just to the west is the Kulturforum, a fine collection of cultural institutions, built in the 1960s as West Berlin's response to East Berlin's Museumsinsel, including the Gemäldegalerie, and its important collections of Old Masters. Adjacent to the Platz is the Tiergarten, Berlin's oldest and most beautiful park.

The Center Potsdamer Platz

MAP PAGE 66, POCKET MAP A15
Potsdamer Str. 4 ⓤ/Ⓢ Potsdamer Platz Ⓦ sonycenter.de. Free.

The striking, eco-friendly, glass-and-steel The Center Potsdamer Platz (formerly the Sony Center), by Helmut Jahn, opened in 2000 and cost a cool €750 million to build. The centre houses shops for everything from cosmetics and jewellery to bikes, plus restaurants, a conference centre, art and film museums, cinemas and a **Legoland** (Ⓦ legolanddiscoverycentre.de). The "Forum", the semi-enclosed roofed space, is used for occasional cultural and entertainment events. There's plenty to do, although the experience is generally soulless and the shopping expensive.

Film and Television Museum

MAP PAGE 66, POCKET MAP A15
Potsdamer Str. 2 ⓤ/Ⓢ Potsdamer Platz Ⓦ deutsche-kinemathek.de. Charge.

One of the must-sees in The Center Potsdamer Platz is the impressively slick **Deutsche Kinemathek** museum, which collects the history of German cinema under one roof. This "journey through film history" explores the pioneering years, silent-film divas, films from the Weimar era, cinema under the Nazis and goes right up to contemporary cinema, with rooms that cover postwar German filmmakers (1946–80) and the present (from 1981). As well as a special exhibit on Germany's biggest star, Marlene Dietrich, there's memorabilia and model film sets from key directors including Fritz Lang and an exhibit that compares East and West German television broadcasts. The museum also organizes the retrospective section of the Berlinale film festival, and hosts special film series, exhibitions and events.

Kollhoff Tower

MAP PAGE 66, POCKET MAP A15
Potsdamer Platz 1 Ⓤ/Ⓢ Potsdamer Platz
Ⓦ panoramapunkt.de. Charge.

Located on the northern edge of Potsdamer Platz, the 25-storey (103m), dark, peat-fired brick Kollhoff Tower is named after architect Hans Kollhoff, a member of the international team of architects (headed by Renzo Piano) that designed many of the buildings for the new Platz. The ground floor houses a number of restaurants and shops, the upper floors are used for office space and – the real highlight – the **Panoramapunkt** on the top floors, offers an open-air viewing platform, reached via Europe's fastest elevator. From the top you can see the Reichstag, Brandenburg Gate, TV Tower, The Center Potsdamer Platz, Tiergarten and Kulturforum. Admission includes entry to the viewing platform, an exhibition on the history of the area, and there's also a café.

The Center Potsdamer Platz

Gemäldegalerie

MAP PAGE 66, POCKET MAP E6
Matthäikirchplatz 4/6 Ⓤ/Ⓢ Potsdamer
Platz Ⓦ smb.museum/museen-
einrichtungen/gemaeldegalerie. Charge.

With a history that goes back to 1830, the Gemäldegalerie holds one of the world's most renowned collections of **classical European painting**. Created from the treasures of the Prussian royalty – including that of Frederick the Great – the collection used to be part of Museum Island (see page 40). The museum – and some of the works – were damaged by Allied bombing during World War II, and the artworks were then split between East and West during the Cold War. After the Wall fell the collection came together again here. Spread across 72 rooms, divided up by country, with sections on Italian, Flemish and Dutch works, the treasures include many high points of European art, with works by Bruegel, a particularly good selection by Cranach, Dürer, Raphael, Rubens, Vermeer and many others. The Rembrandt

room and Caravaggio's exquisite Cupid, *Love Conquers All*, are both must-sees.

Kunstgewerbemuseum

MAP PAGE 66, POCKET MAP E6
Matthäikirchplatz Ⓤ/Ⓢ Potsdamer Platz
Ⓦ smb.museum/museen-einrichtungen/
kunstgewerbemuseum. Charge.

Berlin's Museum of Decorative Arts – one of the oldest in Germany – provides a systematic overview of the key achievements in European design. Over 7000 square metres of white-walled space, the museum covers all major styles and periods, including jaw-dropping silks, tapestries, Renaissance bronzes, contemporary furniture, Rococo glassware, faïence work, porcelain, gold and silver. It includes a Fashion Gallery – which houses around 130 costumes and accessories representing 150 years of fashion history – plus the departments of

Design (think Bauhaus classics mixed with contemporary designers like Philippe Starck and Konstantin Grcic), Jugendstil and Art Deco. A second collection can be found at **Schloss Köpenick** (Schlossinsel 1 Ⓢ Köpenick; charge), a Baroque palace located in a picturesque setting on an island in the river Dahme. Exhibited here are over five hundred items from the sixteenth to eighteenth centuries, as well as Renaissance, Baroque and Rococo furniture and interior decorations.

Kupferstichkabinett

MAP PAGE 66, POCKET MAP E6
Matthäikirchplatz Ⓤ/Ⓢ Potsdamer Platz
Ⓦ smb.museum/en/museums-institutions/
kupferstichkabinett. Charge.

The Kupferstichkabinett, or "print room", is the largest collection of graphic art in Germany, and one of the four most important museums of its kind in the world. The museum houses over 500,000

Potsdamer Platz and Tiergarten

0 metres 500	
0 yards 500	

CAFÉS & BARS
Brammibal's Donuts	7
Café am Neuen See	5
Café Buchwald	2
Kumpelnest 3000	10
Schleusenkrug	4
Victoria Bar	12
Weilands Wellfood	8

RESTAURANTS
Angkor Wat	3
Facil	6
Hugos	9
Joseph Roth Diele	11
Paris-Moskau	1

prints and 110,000 drawings, watercolours, pastels and oil sketches from European artists from the Middle Ages to the present, all on paper. Major artists such as Sandro Botticelli, Albrecht Dürer, Rembrandt, Adolph von Menzel, Pablo Picasso and Andy Warhol are represented. Due to the size and sensitivity of the collection (being largely on paper), there's no permanent display – visitors must check for special exhibitions, or request to see specific artworks via the study room.

Berliner Philharmonie

MAP PAGE 66, POCKET MAP E6
Herbert-von-Karajan-Str. 1 ⓤ /
ⓢ Potsdamer Platz ⓦ berliner-philharmoniker.de. Charge.

Built by architect Hans Scharoun between 1960 and 1963, the Berliner Philharmonie is one of the most important concert halls in Berlin and home to the world-

Kunstgewerbemuseum

renowned **Berlin Philharmonic**. The asymmetrical, tent-like building has an equally distinctive

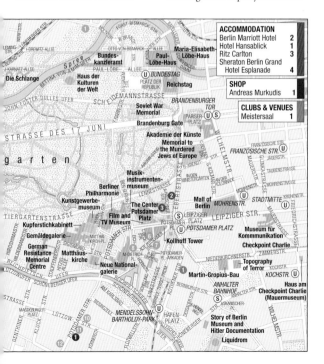

Berliner Philharmonie

pentagon-shaped concert hall (plus a smaller hall, Kammermusiksaal, which seats 1180) that enables great views from all sides. Guided tours of both the Philharmonic Hall and the Chamber Music Hall are available (check website for timings; charge).

Musikinstrumenten-Museum

MAP PAGE 66, POCKET MAP E6
Tiergartenstr. 1 (visitors' entrance Ben-Gurion-Str.) Ⓤ/Ⓢ Potsdamer Platz Ⓦ simpk.de. Charge.
The Musikinstrumenten-Museum embraces Germany's glorious musical history, with over three thousand instruments from the sixteenth to the twenty-first centuries, making it one of the country's largest collections. Many are on permanent display here, including a rare Stradivarius violin, Frederick the Great's flutes, a glass harmonica invented by Benjamin Franklin and – the flamboyant centrepiece – a massive Mighty Wurlitzer theatre organ once owned by the Siemens family, which is demonstrated during **guided tours** (Sat & Thurs; charge). The

museum also veers into electronic music with electric guitars, mixing stations and other experimental instruments, including the Mixtur-Trautonium on which composer Oskar Sala created sound effects for Hitchcock's film *The Birds*.

Neue Nationalgalerie

MAP PAGE 66, POCKET MAP E6
Potsdamer Str. 50 Ⓤ/Ⓢ Potsdamer Platz Ⓦ smb.museum/museen-einrichtungen/ neue-nationalgalerie. Charge.
The "temple of light and glass" (as it is modestly known) and its sculpture gardens were famously designed by Bauhaus affiliate Ludwig Mies van der Rohe. Opened in 1968, the museum houses an extensive collection of twentieth-century European paintings, and sculptures from the nineteenth century to the 1960s, including household names like Bacon, Picasso, Klee, Dix and plenty of German art (E.L. Kirchner, Beckmann). The museum displays portions of its permanent collection on a rotating basis, so each visit is different, and a number of special exhibitions also occur throughout the year, during which

the permanent collection may not be on view. There's also a **café** on the ground floor.

Museum für Kommunikation

MAP PAGE 66, POCKET MAP C15
Leipziger Str. 16 ⓤ Stadtmitte ⓦ mfk-berlin.de. Charge.

Founded in 1872 as the first postal museum of the world, the Museum for Communication experienced a rebirth in 2000, as evidenced by the blue neon writing on the neo-Baroque facade and robots in the lobby. A permanent exhibition showcases the origins, development and future perspectives of the "information society", while highlights of the permanent exhibition are wax seals, postcards and stamps (such as the famous Blue Mauritius), telephones (including some of the first), radios, film, telegraphs and computers. The museum's interactive and lively approach makes it an ideal destination for **kids**, but adults will appreciate the temporary exhibitions featuring cutting-edge artists.

Museum für Kommunikation

The German Resistance Memorial Center

MAP PAGE 66, POCKET MAP D6
Stauffenbergstr. 13–14 (entrance through the commemorative courtyard) ⓤ / ⓢ Potsdamer Platz ⓦ gdw-berlin.de. Free.

Located in a historic section of the former headquarters of the Nazi army high command, the site of the assassination attempt on Adolf Hitler on July 20, 1944, the **Gedenkstätte Deutscher Widerstand** (German Resistance Memorial Center) documents the action taken against the Nazis between 1933 and 1945. The permanent exhibition has over five thousand photographs and documents spread across eighteen topics that go beyond Nazi dissent to address the wider context of resistance, including the role of Christian beliefs in protest, opposition by young people specifically and general defiance of wartime environments in daily life. The memorial courtyard, meanwhile, is dedicated to the conspiring German army officers who were killed after the assassination attempt. The

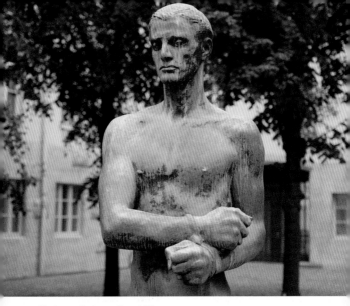

The German Resistance Memorial Center

exhibition is in German and English.

Bauhaus Museum

MAP PAGE 66, POCKET MAP D6
Klingelhöferstr. 14 ⓤ Nollendorfplatz
ⓦ bauhaus.de. The museum is closed for renovation; until it reopens, the Bauhaus Archive will be housed in the Museum für Gestaltung (Knesebeckstr 1-2 ⓤ / ⓢ Zoologischer Garten; charge).
Germany's Bauhaus ("building house") design school may have only lasted from 1919 to 1933 but it went on to become one of the twentieth century's most influential movements – more famous outside the country than Goethe or Schiller. Founded by Walter Gropius, the movement explored the links between fine art and craftsmanship and – a bit later – art and mass production. The **Bauhaus Archive and Museum**, housed in a distinctive building designed by Gropius himself, is the best place to explore the breadth and depth of Bauhaus's expansive activities. Here are tubular steel furniture from Marcel Breuer, armchairs and desks from Mies van der Rohe, paintings from Itten, Schlemmer, Feininger, Albers and Klee… even dapper wallpaper and beautiful chess sets. The museum shop stocks an impressive range of high-quality reproductions, and there's an adjoining café.

Haus der Kulturen der Welt

MAP PAGE 66, POCKET MAP E5
John-Foster-Dulles-Allee 10 ⓤ / ⓢ Bundestag ⓦ hkw.de. Free entry Mon, charge at other times.
Known as the "pregnant oyster" because of its distinctively curvaceous facade, the House of World Cultures hosts exhibitions with a focus on artistic and cultural movements in contemporary global societies. Formerly known as the Kongresshalle conference hall, the building, designed in 1957 by US architect Hugh Stubbins Jr, was a gift from the United States (John F. Kennedy spoke here during his 1963 visit to West Berlin). In 1980 the roof collapsed, injuring many people and killing one, and

was rebuilt in its original style in 1987. The building's maze of rooms includes two exhibition halls, an auditorium for **concerts** and **theatre** and a congress hall, and it is an ideal location for the colourful variety of events held here throughout the year. The eclectic and globally-minded spread of events ranges from educational programmes to exhibitions, music, performing arts, literature festivals and more.

The Tiergarten

MAP PAGE 66, POCKET MAP D5

Full of paths, forested areas, lakes and meadows, the luscious and vast Tiergarten park – bisected by Strasse des 17. Juni – began its life as the preferred hunting ground for the electors of Brandenburg. Designed in its current form in 1830 by landscape architect Peter Joseph Lenne, it is now one of the most relaxing spots in Berlin, and is dotted with a couple of interesting attractions, with the Siegessäule its focal point.

Siegessäule

MAP PAGE 66, POCKET MAP D5
Grosser Stern 1 ⓤ Hansaplatz. Charge.

You can't miss the huge victory column at the centre of the "Grosser Stern" (great star) roundabout in the Tiergarten. The cocksure monument is otherwise known as the-tricky-to-pronounce Siegessäule, built from 1864 to 1873 after a design by Johann Heinrich Stack to commemorate the Prussian victory in the Prusso-Danish war of 1864. It's 69m (25ft) tall, weighs 35 tonnes and features a Goddess of Victory on top, added later after further Prussian victories in wars against Austria and France. At the base you can see bas-reliefs of battles and at the top there's an observatory, which gives great views of the Reichstag, the Brandenburg Gate and the Fernsehturm, but you have to climb the 285 steps to access it. There's also a small **café**, **souvenir shop** and small **exhibition** connecting the column with the events in German history that it represents.

Haus der Kulturen der Welt

Siegessäule

Schloss Bellevue

MAP PAGE 66, POCKET MAP D5
Spreeweg 1 Ⓤ Hansaplatz. Closed to the public.

Situated on an area of 20 hectares (about 50 acres) beside the **River Spree**, Schloss Bellevue was built for Prince August Ferdinand of Prussia, the younger brother of Frederick II of Prussia. The sparkling white home was designed by architect Philipp Daniel Boumann and has the distinction of being the first Neoclassical building constructed in Germany. It was uninhabited in the nineteenth century and used by various institutions such as a museum of ethnography in the 1930s. In 1938, the building was converted into a guesthouse of the government and the entrance to the palace was redesigned. Severely damaged in World War II, it was renovated during 1954–59 and set up as the official residence of the federal president in Berlin. The main sights include a ballroom designed by Carl Gotthard Langhans, the huge lawn behind the palace and the modern building to the south – known as the "presidential egg" due to its oval shape. The palace is currently closed to visitors.

Buchstabenmuseum

MAP PAGE 66, POCKET MAP C4
Stadtbahnbogen 424 Ⓢ Bellevue/ Ⓤ Hansaplatz Ⓦ buchstabenmuseum.de. Charge.

Buchstaben means "letter" (as in "alphabetic character"), and this unique museum – formerly located near Alexanderplatz before moving to this larger space near the Hansaviertel in 2016 – is dedicated solely to the preservation and protection of artisan-esque examples of lettering in the age of digitalization. Though the museum is still building its permanent collection, the assortment of old and new industrial signs is well worth navigating the slightly eccentric opening hours for. Though the museum collects lettering of any language, the ultimate goal is to honour "local colour", which museum founder Barbara Dechant feels is waning.

Shop

Andreas Murkudis

MAP PAGE 66, POCKET MAP E7
Potsdamer Str. 81 ⓤ Kurfürstenstr.
ⓦ andreasmurkudis.com.
Set in the former *Tagesspiegel*
newspaper building, this vast,
white, bright space designed by
lead architects Gonzales Haase is
almost all used to highlight the
high-end (and sometimes pointedly
eccentric) products selected by
Andreas Murkudis, the brother of
fashion designer Kostas Murkudis.
The latter's designs are here, as
are Valextra briefcases and quality
brands like Pringle and Céline.

Restaurants

Angkor Wat

MAP PAGE 66, POCKET MAP D4
Paulstr. 22 ⓤ/Ⓢ Hauptbahnhof
ⓦ angkorwatrestaurant.de.
This cavernous restaurant serves
a mean *yao hon* (Cambodian
fondue). The friendly service
makes up for the exotic decor, and
if you don't like frying your own
meat, the menu extends to other
Cambodian classics with plenty of
spices and creamy coconut. €€€

Facil

MAP PAGE 66, POCKET MAP A15
The Mandala Hotel, Potsdamer Str. 3 ⓤ/
Ⓢ Potsdamer Platz ⓦ facil.de.
Michael Kempf's restaurant in
The Mandala Hotel not only offers
amazing food but also splendid
views from its fifth-floor dining
room, surrounded by a lush
bamboo garden. Popular with
business types, politicos and serious
foodies, Kempf's Michelin-starred,
fish-heavy menu has become justly
famous. €€€€

Hugos

MAP PAGE 66, POCKET MAP C6
Hotel InterContinental, Budapester
Str. 2 ⓤ Zoologischer Garten ⓦ berlin.
intercontinental.com/dine/hugos-
restaurant/.
In a gorgeously appointed
room at the top of the *Hotel
InterContinental*, master
chef Eberhard Lange creates
Michelin-starred "New German–
Mediterranean" food that you
can sample – for a price – while
enjoying the restaurant's panoramic
views. €€€€

Joseph Roth Diele

MAP PAGE 66, POCKET MAP E7
Potsdamer Str. 75 ⓤ Kurfürstenstr.
ⓦ joseph-roth-diele.de.
A splash of charm and colour on
nondescript Potsdamer Strasse,
this quirky, vintage-styled German
restaurant pays homage to interwar
Jewish writer Joseph Roth. The
daily specials are very reasonable,
though the food is homely rather
than high-end. Popular with a wide
range of people at lunchtimes. €

Paris-Moskau

MAP PAGE 66, POCKET MAP E4
Alt-Moabit 141 ⓤ/Ⓢ Hauptbahnhof
ⓦ paris-moskau.de.
This curious mix of old Berlin and
contemporary elegance is set in a

Joseph Roth Diele

nineteenth-century rail signalman's house (it's named after the Paris–Moscow line) and serves hearty meats like ox, fish and dishes like risotto with Alba truffles. It's all backed up by a fine wine list and a great summer garden with views of the government quarter. €€€€

Cafés and bars

Brammibal's Donuts

MAP PAGE 66, POCKET MAP A15
Alte Potsdamer Str. 7 ⓤ/Ⓢ Potsdamer Platz ⓦ brammibalsdonuts.com.
In a town that knows its doughnuts, this 100% vegan spot is up there with the very best. Stores across the city. €

Café am Neuen See

MAP PAGE 66, POCKET MAP C6
Lichtensteinallee 2 ⓤ Zoologischer Garten ⓦ cafeamneuensee.de.
A fine stop-off on any tour of the Tiergarten, this old-school beer garden with modern restaurant (reservations required for larger groups) offers great coffee and draught beers, and a menu including pizza and pasta dishes. It's beautifully set on the Neuen See lake, and there are even rowing boats for rent. €€€€

Café Buchwald

MAP PAGE 66, POCKET MAP C4
Bartningallee 29 ⓤ Hansaplatz ⓦ konditorei-buchwald.de.
A short stroll down a pleasant path from Schloss Bellevue, *Café Buchwald* has been standing here for over 160 years. Not just standing but selling some of the best cakes in town – former suppliers to the court, they still make such delicious confections as home-made *Baumkuchen*. There are a few seats in the charming little front garden. €

Kumpelnest 3000

MAP PAGE 66, POCKET MAP E7
Lützowstr. 23 ⓤ Kurfürstenstr. ⓦ www.kumpelnest3000.com.
Hard to believe that this charming den of iniquity is only a few

A Brammibal's doughnut inspired by a "Maulwurfkuchen" (German mole cake)

Café Buchwald

minutes' stroll from Potsdamer Platz. With its deliberately tacky decor, loyal mixed/gay crowd and anything-goes atmosphere, especially at weekends, it's a good place if you're in the area and looking for the lure of the mirrored disco ball rather than the commercial glare of the Platz.

Schleusenkrug

MAP PAGE 66, POCKET MAP B6
Müller-Breslau-Str. corner Unterschleuse Ⓤ/Ⓢ Zoologischer Garten Ⓦ schleusenkrug.de.
A classic Berlin beer garden, *Schleusenkrug* is a fine place to tuck into a glass of beer and an organic *Wurst*, enjoy a coffee while watching the boats cruise down the canal, or lap up the live music they sometimes have in the summer. €€

Victoria Bar

MAP PAGE 66, POCKET MAP E7
Potsdamer Str. 102 Ⓤ Kurfürstenstr. Ⓦ victoriabar.de.
This much-loved cocktail bar is great for a low-key and decently mixed drink in the week or a livelier atmosphere at weekends. The long bar, subdued lighting and discreet but upbeat music create a decent buzz.

Weilands Wellfood

MAP PAGE 66, POCKET MAP A15
Marlene-Dietrich-Platz 1 Ⓤ/Ⓢ Potsdamer Platz Ⓦ weilands-wellfood.de.
Right by a pond near bustling Potsdamer Platz, this health-conscious, fast-food-style store sells food low in calories and high in vitamins: couscous, salads, curries and sandwiches stacked with fresh ingredients. Popular with local workers at lunchtimes. €€

Clubs and venues

Meistersaal

MAP PAGE 66, POCKET MAP F6
Köthener Str. 38 Ⓤ/Ⓢ Potsdamer Platz Ⓦ meistersaal-berlin.de.
This hundred-year-old music venue and recording studio has drawn major artists from Kurt Tucholsky and David Bowie to U2 and Herbert Grönemeyer. Built in 1913 in what was once Berlin's music quarter, the building fell into disrepair after World War II. Since then, though, the Meistersaal has become Berlin's version of London's Abbey Road, world-renowned for its excellent acoustics.

Prenzlauer Berg and Wedding

Built in the nineteenth century as a working-class district, Prenzlauer Berg was neglected by the GDR after World War II, becoming a crumbling ghetto for intellectuals, punks and bohemians. Following merciless post-Wall gentrification, wealthy creative types and middle-class families have gravitated here, drawn by the area's handsome, cobbled streets, leafy squares like Helmholtzplatz and Kollwitzplatz, and its distinctive Alt Berlin atmosphere, with lots of independent bars and cafés, Kastanienallee's boutiques and the buzzy Sunday flea market at Mauerpark. While Prenzlauer Berg's nightlife has been reduced to a few late-night bars, just over the famous Bösebrücke – where the Bornholmer Strasse border crossing was first officially breached in November 1989 – lies the former Western district of Wedding. Known for its large immigrant population and edgy charm, this up-and-coming borough is peppered with the kind of underground spaces that were once common in Prenzlauer Berg during the 1990s.

Gedenkstätte Berliner Mauer

MAP PAGE 78, POCKET MAP G2
Bernauer Str. 111–119 ⓤ Bernauer Str./
ⓢ Nordbahnhof ⓦ berliner-mauer-gedenkstaette.de. Free.

Based slightly away from the tourist centre, so avoiding the crowds that throng Checkpoint Charlie, the Berlin Wall Memorial takes a more academic look at Germany's division. A section of the former border strip is the focus for the **memorial**, while an outdoor exhibition on the former death-strip shows the history of Bernauer Strasse and the Wall itself. Stretching 1.4km up to the Mauerpark, it includes traces of border obstacles that retain the appearance of the Wall as it would have been at the time.

The **museum** opposite, expanded in 2014, now hosts a permanent exhibition ("1961–1989: the Berlin Wall"), which documents the lives of those attempting to escape the dictatorship (the most successful escape tunnels were dug near here) and the resistance efforts – sometimes fatal – organized by those living nearby. There's also a separate exhibition on the division of the U-Bahn and S-Bahn lines displayed in the adjacent **Nordbahnhof** station (open during station opening hours). Prayer services for the victims of the Berlin Wall are held in the **chapel** on weekdays at noon.

Mauerpark Flohmarkt

MAP PAGE 78, POCKET MAP H2
Bernauer Str. 63–65 ⓤ Bernauer Str.
ⓦ flohmarktimmauerpark.de. Free.

The Mauerpark flea market is a city institution, a popular Sunday stop for hungover students, bargain hunters, families and shade-wearing clubbers who come to scan the international food stalls, clothes shops and nostalgic bric-a-brac that seems to extend forever. You can find everything here from

Kollwitzplatz

bike parts, 1950s cutlery sets and faded jigsaws to new and vintage clothes, GDR memorabilia, record players and lots of vinyl and CDs. As with most flea markets, there's a decent amount of what might uncharitably be called "junk" but also some genuine antiques. Adjacent to the market you'll find the actual **Mauerpark**, a strip of landscaped green that was once the site of a stretch of Berlin Wall and the associated death strip, loomed over by the Friedrich-Ludwig-Jahn-Sportpark and the Max-Schmeling-Halle. In warm weather, check out the weekly karaoke session in the "bearpit", which attracts massive crowds from 2.30/3pm.

Kollwitzplatz

MAP PAGE 78, POCKET MAP J2
Kollwitzplatz ⓤ Eberswalder Str./ Senefelderplatz.

Kollwitzplatz is one of Prenzlauer Berg's best-known and most attractive squares. It was named after artist Käthe Kollwitz (1867–1945), who lived in the area at the turn of the twentieth century (a simple plaque commemorates her former home on Kollwitzstr.) and whose squat, serious-looking **sculpture** is one of the main features of the square. From the appearance of the lavishly restored facades it is hard to tell that Kollwitzplatz was once one of Berlin's poorest areas, but Kollwitz's work (see page 124) reveals the area to have once been home to the city's more impoverished and downtrodden citizens. This was one of the first areas to be gentrified when the Wall fell in 1989 and today symbolizes Prenzlauer Berg's yuppie status as well as its bias towards families (some call this part of the city Pramzlauerberg). It's a lovely place to come for a stroll – three **playgrounds** and a leafy **park** lie within the square, and endless restaurants, cafés and smart boutiques are scattered around its perimeter. Saturdays are especially popular thanks to the extensive **farmers' market**, offering everything from organic meat and fish, fruit and veg, sweets and coffee and clothes. A smaller (and less crowded) organic market also takes place on Thursdays. In summer especially the fun carries on till late at night.

Prenzlauer Berg

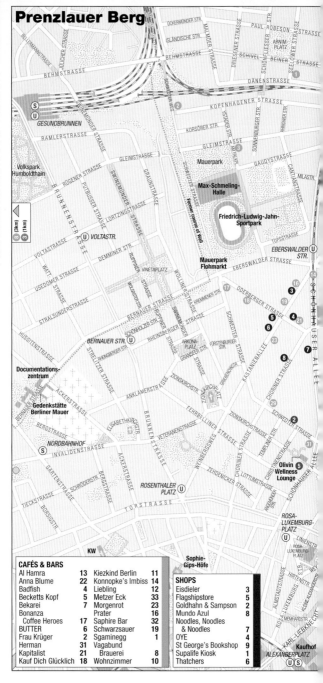

CAFÉS & BARS			
Al Hamra	13	Kiezkind Berlin	11
Anna Blume	22	Konnopke's Imbiss	14
Badfish	4	Liebling	12
Becketts Kopf	5	Metzer Eck	33
Bekarei	7	Morgenrot	23
Bonanza		Prater	16
Coffee Heroes	17	Saphire Bar	32
BUTTER	6	Schwarzsauer	19
Frau Krüger	2	Sgameingg	1
Herman	31	Vagabund	
Kapitalist	21	Brauerei	8
Kauf Dich Glücklich	18	Wohnzimmer	10

SHOPS	
Eisdieler	3
Flagshipstore	5
Goldhahn & Sampson	2
Mundo Azul	8
Noodles, Noodles	
& Noodles	4
OYE	7
St George's Bookshop	9
Supalife Kiosk	1
Thatchers	6

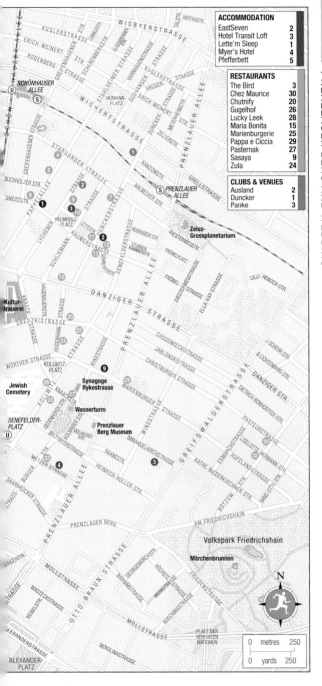

ACCOMMODATION

EastSeven	2
Hotel Transit Loft	3
Lette'm Sleep	1
Myer's Hotel	4
Pfefferbett	5

RESTAURANTS

The Bird	3
Chez Maurice	30
Chutnify	20
Gugelhof	26
Lucky Leek	28
Maria Bonita	15
Marienburgerie	25
Pappa e Ciccia	29
Pasternak	27
Sasaya	9
Zula	24

CLUBS & VENUES

Ausland	2
Duncker	1
Panke	3

Jewish cemetery

MAP PAGE 78, POCKET MAP J2

Schönhauser Allee 23–25

ⓤ Senefelderplatz ⓦ jg-berlin.org. Free.

A short hop from the
Senefelderplatz U-Bahn, Prenzlauer
Berg's small but charming Jewish
cemetery (Jüdischer Friedhof)
was built to cater for the overspill
from the one on Mitte's Grosse
Hamburger Strasse. It was mostly
used between 1827 and 1880, at a
time when the Jewish population
in this area was thriving, and holds
approximately 22,000 graves and
almost a thousand hereditary
family plots, including the graves
of painter Max Liebermann, the
publisher Leopold Ullstein, the
composer Giacomo Meyerbeer
and German-Jewish banker Joseph
Mendelssohn (son of the influential
philosopher Moses Mendelssohn).
Sadly many gravestones, the original
cemetery entrance and mourning
chapel were destroyed during World
War II and subsequent anti-Semitic
vandalism – and many graves are
still in a dilapidated state, some
riddled with bullet holes. The
cemetery was rebuilt in the 1960s,
and the adjacent lapidarium – on
the site of the former mourning
hall – was opened in 2004 as a place
to preserve and protect sixty of the
most valuable stones, as well as to
display panels on Jewish culture and
Jewish mourning rituals. Note that
men are obliged to cover their heads
to visit the cemetery: hats can be
borrowed from the lapidarium but
visitors are urged to bring their own.

Synagoge Rykestrasse

MAP PAGE 78, POCKET MAP J2

Rykestr. 53 ⓤ Senefelderstr. ⓦ jg-berlin.
org. Open for services only.

Built by Johann Hoeniger at the
turn of the twentieth century, this
gorgeous Neoclassical synagogue
(inaugurated in 1904) is one of
Germany's largest – and one of
Berlin's loveliest. The building
survived *Kristallnacht* in 1938
as it was located between
"Aryan" apartment buildings,
although precious Torah scrolls
were damaged and rabbis and
congregation members were
deported to Sachsenhausen (see
page 136). The synagogue was
also used as stables during the
war, but was finally restored to its
former glory by architects Ruth
Golan and Kay Zareh in 2007, who
used black-and-white photographs
and a €6-million budget to lavishly
re-create the remarkable original.
Outside of service times, the
synagogue can only be visited via
prior arrangement.

The Wasserturm

MAP PAGE 78, POCKET MAP J2

Corner of Knaackstr. & Rykestr.

ⓤ Eberswalder Str./Senefelderplatz.

Designed by Henry Gill,
constructed by the English
Waterworks Company and finished
in 1877, the 30m-high cylindrical
brick water tower, known as
"Dicker Hermann", has become
one of Prenzlauer Berg's unofficial
symbols. Among the oldest of its
kind in the city, it was one of the
first places to provide running
water in the country and remained

Mauerpark Flohmarkt

in use until the 1950s. Its engine house was used as an unofficial prison by the SA in 1933–45 – 28 bodies were later found in the underground pipe network, and a commemorative plaque stands outside on Knaackstrasse. During GDR times the tower was used to store canned fish, which could apparently be smelled across the whole neighbourhood. The building was then abandoned and became a "playground" for local kids. Today the refurbished tower is home to much-coveted cake-wedge-shaped apartments (formerly belonging to the tower's operators), while the underground reservoir space hosts sporadic cultural events.

Olivin Wellness Lounge

MAP PAGE 78, POCKET MAP J3
Schönhauser Allee 177 ⓤ Senefelderplatz
ⓦ olivin-berlin.com. Charge.
With its exposed brick walls, **saunas** and an excellent bamboo garden, this Finnish sauna is a great way to unwind whatever the season. Special offers are available in winter; massages are available as extra during a four-hour sauna session.

Kulturbrauerei

MAP PAGE 78, POCKET MAP J2
Schönhauser Allee 36 (entrance on Sredzkistr.) ⓤ Eberswalder Str.
ⓦ kulturbrauerei.de. Free for main complex, charge specific venues.
This lovely, sprawling, red-and-yellow brick complex dates to 1842, when it was a small brewery and pub. It was expanded to its current size after 1880. Since the late 1990s, it's been one of Prenzlauer Berg's major commercial hubs, with offices, bars, restaurants, clubs and an eight-theatre cinema (Kino in der KulturBrauerei; ⓦ cinestar.de).
As well as the cinema and shops, the weekly street food market (every Sunday) and Scandinavian Christmas market (end of November to end of December) are worth a visit, as is the **Museum**

in der Kulturbrauerei (Knaackstr. 97; hdg.de/museum-in-der-kulturbrauerei; free) – opened 2013 – whose permanent exhibition, "Everyday Life in the GDR", documents East German cultural history. The Kesselhaus concert hall hosts some decent indie rock and pop shows. You can also pick up guided cycle tours (March–Nov; ⓦ berlinonbike.de).

Museum Pankow

MAP PAGE 78, POCKET MAP J3
Prenzlauer Allee 227–228
ⓤ Senefelderplatz ⓣ 030 90 29 53 917. Free.
Spread across the first floor of a former school, this small but lively museum documents the history of the district and its working-class inhabitants from the nineteenth century to today. The permanent exhibition consists mainly of photos and texts (German only) displayed along corridors, though a couple of large rooms and a separate building across the courtyard occasionally host more modern, multimedia exhibitions on themes such as the evolution of lesbian, gay and transgender life in the area.

Zeiss-Grossplanetarium

MAP PAGE 78, POCKET MAP K1
Prenzlauer Allee 80 Ⓢ Prenzlauer Allee
ⓦ planetarium.berlin. Charge.
A massive building set back from bustling **Prenzlauer Allee**, the Zeiss Planetarium was built in 1987. At the time, it was one of Europe's largest and most modern stellar theatres, with a giant, golf ball-esque silver dome measuring 23m across. Reopened in early 2016, its auditorium still contains a digital projection of Earth's starry skies into the roof, but the program of astronomical, science, film and music events are more cutting edge, as well as entertaining and educational. Many of the shows are multilingual too (English, Spanish, French).

Shops

Eisdieler

MAP PAGE 78, POCKET MAP J2
Kastanienallee 12 Ⓤ Eberswalder Strasse
Ⓦ eisdieler.de.

Contemporary fashion design for men – clothing and accessories – including brands like Qwstion, Onitsuka Tiger, Spring Court and Schmoove. Good selection of vintage sunglasses.

Flagshipstore

MAP PAGE 78, POCKET MAP H2
Oderberger Str. 53 Ⓤ Eberswalder Str.
Ⓦ flagshipstore-berlin.de.

Representing dozens of Berlin's fashion labels and international designers, Flagshipstore offers a vast range of contemporary clothing and accessories for women and men.

Goldhahn & Sampson

MAP PAGE 78, POCKET MAP J1
Dunckerstr. 9 Ⓤ Eberswalder Str.
Ⓦ goldhahnundsampson.de.

A foodies' paradise that houses a vast spread of condiments, spices and other tasty delicacies from all over the world, plus cookbooks and utensils. It holds regular wine tasting and cookery courses, and there are other locations at Wilmersdorfer Str. 102 (Ⓤ Wilmersdorfer Str.) and in Kreuzberg's Markthalle Neun (Ⓤ Görlitzer Bahnhof).

Mundo Azul

MAP PAGE 78, POCKET MAP J2
Choriner Str. 49 Ⓤ Senefelderplatz
Ⓦ mundoazul.de.

"Blue world" is a children's and illustration bookstore that stocks beautiful books in French, Spanish, German and English, and also runs events and exhibitions (check online for details).

Noodles, Noodles & Noodles

MAP PAGE 78, POCKET MAP J2
Schönhauser Allee 156 Ⓤ Eberswalder Str.
Ⓦ noodles.de.

Despite its slightly under-the-radar location, this store is worth seeking out for its handsome furniture, made using old-school artisanal

Mundo Azul

techniques and high-quality materials – built to last.

OYE

MAP PAGE 78, POCKET MAP J2
Oderberger Str. 4 Ⓤ Eberswalder Str.
Ⓦ oye-records.com.
Originally catering for collectors of Latin, soul and funk vinyl, OYE now covers an impressive range of styles, from Afrobeat to Berlin club staples, house and techno.

St George's Bookshop

MAP PAGE 78, POCKET MAP J2
Wörther Str. 27 Ⓤ Eberswalder
Str. or tram #M2 to Marienburger
Ⓦ saintgeorgesbookshop.com.
Founded in 2003 by British twins Paul and Daniel, this delightful shop sells a fine selection of new and used English-language books. There's a sofa to chill on, free wi-fi and they'll buy your used books.

Supalife Kiosk

MAP PAGE 78, POCKET MAP J1
Raumerstr. 40 Ⓤ Eberswalder Str.
Ⓦ supalife.de.
This small boutique sells the wares of Berlin urban artists, from comics and fanzines to silkscreen prints and paintings. They're well connected to some of the city's best-known artists so expect special one-offs too.

Thatchers

MAP PAGE 78, POCKET MAP H2
Kastanienallee 21 Ⓤ Eberswalder Str.
Ⓦ thatchers.de.
Upmarket fashion store for women who like their dresses, skirts and shirts classy and sexy without ever being over the top. A perfect place to pick up sensual evening dresses, sophisticated club wear and also savvy gifts.

Restaurants

The Bird

MAP PAGE 78, POCKET MAP H1
Am Falkplatz 5 Ⓤ/Ⓢ Schönhauser Allee

Ⓦ thebirdinberlin.com.
This no-nonsense New York-style steakhouse is famed for its large and tasty burgers, spicy chicken wings and casual ambience. With the neon bar, exposed brickwork and US accents it's a bit like being on the set of *Cheers*. A great place to fill up cheaply and sip on a cold beer. €€

Chez Maurice

MAP PAGE 78, POCKET MAP L3
Bötzowstr. 39 Ⓢ Greifswalder Str. Ⓦ chez-maurice.com.
One of the finer dining spots in the quietly upmarket Bötzowviertel, *Maurice* is an intimate, rustic place offering high-quality seasonal French dishes – they'll even take requests with enough notice – and an expansive wine list (over two hundred from France alone). €€€

Chutnify

MAP PAGE 78, POCKET MAP J2
Szredki Str. 43 Ⓤ Eberswalderstr.
Ⓦ chutnify.com.
Single-handedly challenging Berlin's dire reputation for mediocre, spice-avoiding Indian food, *Chutnify* specializes in South Indian street food with an emphasis on delicious *dosas*, crispy lentil crêpes and spicy *chai* teas. Designed by owner Aparna Aurora, it looks good too, with colourful furnishings and outside seating in summer. A second branch can be found at Pflügerstr. 25 (Ⓤ Hermannplatz). €€

Gugelhof

MAP PAGE 78, POCKET MAP J2
Knaackstr. 37, cnr Kollwitzplatz
Ⓤ Senefelderplatz/Eberswalder Str.
Ⓦ gugelhof.com.
A Kollwitzplatz classic, *Gugelhof* has been serving consistently good Alsatian food since the Wall fell, and counts Bill Clinton among its many dignified diners. It's a surprisingly down-to-earth place, with friendly staff and robust

yet refined cuisine that includes *Flammkuchen* (*tarte flambée*) and pork knuckle. Reservations recommended. €€€

Lucky Leek

MAP PAGE 78, POCKET MAP J2
Kollwitzstr. 54 ⓊSenefelderplatz Ⓦlucky-leek.com.
This high-end vegan spot occupies a smart space inside an old building on one of Prenzlauer Berg's loveliest streets. The menu is inventive and service excellent, but you'll certainly pay above average for the experience. €€€€

Maria Bonita

MAP PAGE 78, POCKET MAP J2
Danziger Str. 33 ⓊEberswalder Str. Ⓦmariabonita.de.
Tucked away amidst the slew of *imbisses* and kebab shops that make up much of this part of Danziger Strasse, *Maria Bonita* stands out for its above-average street-style Mexican food. You couldn't swing an enchilada inside, but the burritos, tacos and *quesadillas* – and the guacamole for that matter – are excellent value for money. €

Marienburgerie

MAP PAGE 78, POCKET MAP K2
Marienburger Str. 47; tram #M2 to Marienburger Str. Ⓦmarienburgerie.de.
This diminutive but buzzy burger hangout lures locals back again and again with huge, delicious beef, chicken, fish or vegetarian burgers (the Marienburger is almost too big to eat in one sitting). Organic options also available. €

Pappa e Ciccia

MAP PAGE 78, POCKET MAP H2
Schwedter Str. 18 ⓊSenefelderplatz Ⓦpappaeciccia.de.
Smart, modern restaurant serving Italian classics made using local ingredients. It's all organic and there are decent vegetarian and vegan options. Ice cream, cakes and more on offer at the adjacent organic deli. €€€€

Pasternak

MAP PAGE 78, POCKET MAP J2
Knaackstr. 22–24 ⓊSenefelderplatz Ⓦrestaurant-pasternak.de.
This long-standing Russian/Jewish restaurant, named after the author of *Doctor Zhivago*, is best known for its incredible Sunday brunch: a regal spread of blini, caviar, fish and much more, it's so popular you'll need to get there early (no reservations). The same proprietors run a decent Israeli restaurant over the road (directly opposite the synagogue) called – get it? – *Masel Topf* (Ⓦrestaurant-maseltopf.de). €€€

Sasaya

MAP PAGE 78, POCKET MAP J1
Lychener Str. 50 Ⓤ/ⓈSchönhauser Allee Ⓦsasaya-berlin.de.
Bucking the trend for catch-all pan-Asian menus, *Sasaya* focuses on serving traditional and innovative Japanese food. The quality and freshness of the ingredients is high, the food is delicious and service is swift – a serious contender for best sushi spot in the city. €€€

Zula

MAP PAGE 78, POCKET MAP J2
Husemann Str. 10 ⓊSenefelderplatz Ⓦzulaberlin.com.
The humble chickpea dish reaches superlative status at this cosy, Israeli-run hummus spot. Visitors can stick with a traditional hummus plate or try out the *hummus shakshuka* and even *hummus goulash* – all of it is delicious. Home-made pitta bread and a nice wine list seal the deal. €

Cafés and bars

Al Hamra

MAP PAGE 78, POCKET MAP J1
Raumerstr. 16 ⓊEberswalder Strasse Ⓦalhamra.de.
Comfortable Middle Eastern café with shabby décor but decent Mediterranean food, beer, backgammon and chess. €

Anna Blume

MAP PAGE 78, POCKET MAP J2
Kollwitzstr. 83 Ⓤ Eberswalder Str. Ⓦ cafe-anna-blume.de.

Part flower shop, part café and part bakery, this Art Deco classic – named after a Kurt Schwitters poem, whose lines are elegantly inscribed on the walls inside – is one of the area's best-known cafés. Slide into one of the red leather banquettes and sample one of their superb cakes, or try a refined tiered breakfast platter. €€

Badfish

MAP PAGE 78, POCKET MAP J1
Stargarder Str. 14 Ⓤ/Ⓢ Schönhauser Allee Ⓦ badfishbarberlin.com.

This New York-style neighbourhood bar has become an in-spot for expats and natives alike. Smokey and boisterous (especially at weekends), and with a hip selection of sounds on the jukebox, friendly staff and an excellent array of craft beers, whiskeys and shots, it makes for an almost guaranteed fun night out. "Angry hour" between 5–7pm and free popcorn at all times.

Becketts Kopf

MAP PAGE 78, POCKET MAP J1
Pappelallee 64 Ⓤ/Ⓢ Schönhauser Allee Ⓦ becketts-kopf.de.

It's easy to walk straight past this deliberately clandestine cocktail bar – but you'd be missing out. Look out for the glowering head of Mr Beckett staring at you from the darkness and enter to find a sophisticated and intimate space with one of the best cocktail lists in town.

Bekarei

MAP PAGE 78, POCKET MAP J1
Dunker Str. 23 Ⓢ Prenzlauer Allee Ⓦ bekarei.com.

This Greek-Portuguese bakery is a firm local favourite thanks to its freshly baked breads, pretzels, cakes and pastries. The interior is colourfully retro, the staff are friendlier than usual and menu items of note include pancakes, flakey *tiropitakia* and *pastel de nata*. Note that it gets particularly busy with families at weekends. €

Bonanza Coffee Heroes

MAP PAGE 78, POCKET MAP H2

Zula

Oderberger Str. 35 Ⓤ Bernauer Str./
Eberswalder Str. Ⓦ bonanzacoffee.de.
Coffee connoisseurs flock to
Bonanza to sample the wares of
their famed baristas: perfect lattes
and flat whites knocked up on a
fancy Slayer Espresso machine.
Single origin filter coffees also
served; more locations across the
city, including the roastery in
Kreuzberg (Adalbertstr. 70). €

BUTTER

MAP PAGE 78, POCKET MAP J1
Pappelallee. 73 Ⓤ Eberswalder Strasse
Ⓦ cafe-butter.de.
Smart place for excellent breakfasts
and brunches, great and small.
Inventive vegetarian and vegan
plates and superb pancakes. €

Frau Krüger

MAP PAGE 78, POCKET MAP H1
Kopenhagener Str. 37 Ⓤ Schönhauser Allee
Ⓦ cafe-fraukrueger.de.
A simple but friendly and cute
café just off Mauerpark, one of the
best places to come after a day in
the park or when you are ready to
get some of their famous frozen
yoghurt, having spent the morning
at the flea market. The friendly

Kapitalist

staff makes having coffee, cake,
breakfast or brunch here even
nicer. €

Herman

MAP PAGE 78, POCKET MAP F10
Schönhauser Allee 173 Ⓤ Senefelderplatz
Ⓦ herman.berlin.
Located along the busy section of
Schönhauser Allee that links Mitte
with Prenzlauer Berg, this Belgian-
themed bar – run by welcoming
and knowledgeable owner Bart
Neirynck – has an incredibly broad
selection of beers. It's a great place
to start the night, but chances are
you'll end up staying for longer
than planned.

Kapitalist

MAP PAGE 78, POCKET MAP J2
Oderberger Str. 2 Ⓤ Eberswalder Str.
☎ 030 47 37 44 860.
Kapitalist is a much less anti-
establishment place than its beaten-
up facade suggests – it attracts a
friendly, bubbly crowd of locals
who come for coffees and people-
watching in the day and beer and
wine at night.

Kauf Dich Glücklich

MAP PAGE 78, POCKET MAP H2
Oderberger Str. 44 Ⓤ Bernauer Str./
Eberswalder Str. Ⓦ kaufdichgluecklich.de.
Come here for waffles, ice cream
– and a spot of cutely kitsch
capitalism. "Buy yourself happy"
is an irrepressibly cheerful place
where you can not only get great
coffee and sweet treats but also buy
any of the secondhand furniture
– tables, chairs, lamps, sunglasses –
you see around you. €

Kiezkind Berlin

MAP PAGE 78, POCKET MAP J1
Helmholtzplatz Ⓤ Eberswalderstr. ☎ 030
40 05 78 50.
Located right on leafy
Helmholtzplatz, this large, family-
oriented café is an ideal place to
take a break with the little ones.
Inside, they can play with the
abundant toys or in the sandpit, or

Anna Blume

ride around on the tricycles outside while you enjoy a well-made latte and slice of cake from the counter. Regular family-friendly flea markets also. €

Konnopke's Imbiss

MAP PAGE 78, POCKET MAP J1
Schönhauser Allee 44b Ⓤ Eberswalder Str.
Ⓦ konnopke-imbiss.de.
This legendary stand has been serving up Berlin street snacks – *Currywurst*, *pommes frites*, *Bratwurst* – since 1930. Incredibly it's been run by the same family all that time – perfect for a quick bite. It's perfect for a quick bite any time of day; if you want to feel like a local, eat your food standing up at one of the tables outside. €

Liebling

MAP PAGE 78, POCKET MAP J1
Raumerstr. 36 Ⓢ Prenzlauer Allee/
Ⓤ Eberswalder Str. Ⓦ cafeliebling.berlin.
You'll find this attractive café on the corner of Dunckerstrasse and Raumerstrasse. Inside is a subtly cool interior, great cakes and decent lunch options (soups, quiches). The good wine and beer, and the *au courant* music on the system, make it popular in the evenings too. €

Metzer Eck

MAP PAGE 78, POCKET MAP F10
Metzer Str. 33 Ⓤ Eberswalder Str.
Ⓦ metzer-eck.de.
The oldest inn in Prenzlauer Berg (1913) inevitably packs plenty of old-school charm. It's faded slightly since its days as a major meeting point for Prenzlauer Berg's more bohemian contingent in the GDR, but still serves a decent Pilsner and delicious *Bolettes* (meatballs) and *Bockwurst*. €

Morgenrot

MAP PAGE 78, POCKET MAP H2
Kastanienallee 85 Ⓤ Eberswalder Str.
Ⓦ cafe-morgenrot.de.
Kastanienallee's best-known alternative café is located right next to an immense squat (one of the last in the area). Despite the anticapitalist slogans and punk aura, it's a friendly, open place that serves up a good weekend vegan breakfast. €

Prater

MAP PAGE 78, POCKET MAP J2
Kastanienallee 7–9 Ⓤ Eberswalder Str.
Ⓦ pratergarten.de.
Dating back to 1837, *Prater* is the city's oldest beer garden and remains a fantastic place for a

taste of traditional Berlin boozing, especially during summer when people swarm around the long tables and snack kiosks. During winter, it's all about feasting on homemade Berlin cuisine inside the classic interior.

Saphire Bar

MAP PAGE 78, POCKET MAP L3
Bötzowstr. 31 ⑤ Greifswalder Str.
Ⓦ saphirebar.de.
The *Saphire Bar* mixes together its whisky and cocktail bar credentials as well as it mixes its drinks, with two elegant lounges to enjoy a cultivated yet unpretentious evening in.

Schwarzsauer

MAP PAGE 78, POCKET MAP J2
Kastanienallee 13 Ⓤ Eberswalder Str.
Ⓣ 030 44 85 633.
"Black and Sour" lives up to its name with its moody service, average food and smoky, plain interior. Still, it has a certain Berlin-esque atmosphere that makes it decidedly popular.

The Duncker club

Sgaminegg

MAP PAGE 78, POCKET MAP J1
Seelower Str. 2 Ⓤ/Ⓢ Schönhauser Allee
Ⓦ sgaminegg.de.
There is a dearth of decent cafés north of Stargarderstrasse, but *Sgaminegg* is an absolute treasure thanks to delicious coffees, homemade lunches – couscous, lentil and south German dishes – and a little shop that sells local produce. Check out the website on the day for daily specials. €

Vagabund Brauerei

MAP PAGE 78, POCKET MAP C1
Antwerpener Str. 3 Ⓤ Seestrasse
Ⓦ vagabundbrauerei.com.
One of Europe's first crowd-sourced breweries, *Vagabund* is run by three American friends with a highly infectious passion for craft beer. As well as their own excellent brews, they sell classic Belgian ales and lager from family breweries in southern Germany, all in a welcoming, unpretentious atmosphere that draws locals and expats alike.

Liebling

Wohnzimmer

MAP PAGE 78, POCKET MAP J1
Lettestr. 6 Ⓤ **Eberswalder Str.**
Ⓦ **wohnzimmer-bar.de.**
This retro, elegant "living room" is
a local institution. One of the first
spots to champion flea-market chic,
it serves as both a relaxed daytime
café and amiable spot for a late
night drink later on. At weekends
a cocktail bar magically pops up
between its two rooms.

Clubs and venues

Ausland

MAP PAGE 78, POCKET MAP J1
Lychener Str. 60 Ⓢ **Prenzlauer Allee**
Ⓦ **ausland-berlin.de.**
One for the experimentalists,
Ausland is a nonprofit club
committed to promoting music,
performance and related events.
You can find anything from free
jazz and sound-art gigs to movies
and installations, all of which take
place in an undecorated bunker
in front of an apartment block.

Unlike most places, door fees go
directly to the artists.

Duncker

MAP PAGE 78, POCKET MAP K1
Dunckerstr. 64 Ⓢ **Prenzlauer Allee**
Ⓦ **dunckerclub.de.**
Duncker touches the musical
parts other Prenzlauer Berg clubs
don't reach, thanks to a mix of
new wave and indie nights and
particularly its weekly "Dark
Mondays" – one of the city's few
goth/industrial nights. Aptly
enough, it's located in a striking
neo-Gothic church.

Panke

MAP PAGE 78, POCKET MAP E1
Gerichtstr. 23 Ⓢ **Wedding** Ⓦ **pankeculture.
com.**
This alternative cultural hub, run
by a group of friends, is hidden
away in a network of run-down
industrial courtyards. Expect
underground DJ nights, which
veer from hip-hop and soul to
world and funk (never techno),
plus film nights and a decent café.

Friedrichshain

Though part of an ensemble of former East inner-city areas, Friedrichshain has developed a slightly different mien than that of neighbouring Mitte and Prenzlauer Berg. A magnet for lefties, anarchists and students, it has managed to resist the same levels of gentrification thanks to an organized squatter scene, activist demos and the occasional car-burning frenzy. That said, its defiantly unkempt environs have succumbed to an invasion of bars and cafés around Boxhagener Platz and an encroaching media presence along the river. It's most popular for bar-hopping, clubbing and cheap midnight snacking, but the area does offer some heavyweight public monuments, the world-famous East Side Gallery and the imposing Karl-Marx-Allee among them. It's also home to – indeed named after – the lovely, sprawling Volkspark Friedrichshain.

Volkspark Friedrichshain

MAP PAGE 92, POCKET MAP K3

Ⓤ **Strausberger Platz/Weberwiese.** Established 150 years ago to commemorate the centenary of Frederick the Great's accession

to the throne, Volkspark Friedrichshain is one of Berlin's oldest parks. Casually straddling the boroughs of Prenzlauer Berg and Friedrichshain, it's a sprawling place featuring lots of recreational

Volkspark Friedrichshain

Karl-Marx-Allee

opportunities (tennis courts, volleyball nets and climbing walls) and a wealth of impressive monuments. Highlights include the **Märchenbrunnen**, a neo-Baroque fountain built at the turn of the twentieth century, memorials to Frederick the Great, the German antifascist groups of World War II and a **peace bell** given to East Berlin by Japan. The park's two main hills (the 78m Grosse Bunkerberg and the 48m Kleine Bunkerberg) were constructed with rubble from the war. The park also has a café and a summertime open-air cinema.

East Side Gallery

MAP PAGE 92, POCKET MAP L6
Mühlenstr. 1 ⓦ Warschauer Str.
ⓦ **eastsidegallery-berlin.com. 24hr.**
This 1.3km-long section of the Berlin Wall by the Spree is purportedly the largest open-air gallery in the world and one of the city's best-known landmarks. Painted in 1990 (on the east side) when the Wall fell, the gallery features works from over a hundred artists from all over the world. Over the years it has fallen victim

to vandalism and erosion, hence a controversial decision to repaint it in time for the twentieth-anniversary celebrations in 2009. The East Side Gallery made the news again in 2013 when a section was removed to make way for some luxury apartments; the resulting outcry drew ten thousand protesters and an impromptu appearance by David Hasselhoff. Since 2016 a **museum** close to the Oberbaumbrücke (see page 93) end of the Wall (Mühlenstr. 78-80 ⓦ thewallmuseum.com; charge) tells the story of the Wall years through a multimedia presentation that includes over 100 screens, interactive displays, original newsreel footage and filmed interviews with border guards.

Karl-Marx-Allee

MAP PAGE 92, POCKET MAP L5
ⓤ **Frankfurter Tor/Strausberger Platz.**
The monumental Karl-Marx-Allee, as the name suggests, is a thoroughly Communist phenomenon. Built between 1952 and 1960, the imposing 89m-wide, 2km-long street – book-ended by German architect Hermann

Henselmann's tiered "wedding cake" towers at Frankfurter Tor and Strausberger Platz – was originally named Grosse Frankfurter Strasse and later Stalinallee. The idea was to build luxurious apartments for workers (they were inevitably doled out to party officials) as well as a leisure area featuring shops, restaurants, cafés and the still-standing Kino International. On June 17, 1953, the street was the focus of worker demonstrations; at least 125 people died in the brutal suppression by Soviet forces that followed. Since reunification most of the buildings have been restored and the apartments converted into upmarket flats and offices. The vast dimensions of the street and its run of blocky Soviet architecture make it a fantastic place for a stroll – the spaces between buildings are scaled up beyond the norm, so you may be clocking up more miles than you realize. Stop off at *Café Sybille* (see page 96), which hosts a small but insightful museum on the street's history.

Computerspielemuseum

MAP PAGE 92, POCKET MAP L5
Karl-Marx-Allee 93a Ⓤ Weberwiese
Ⓦ computerspielemuseum.de. Charge.
The world's first-ever **computer game museum** is a fun and highly interactive tribute to gaming, featuring pretty much every kind of arcade machine and games console ever made, from the pioneering Nimrod (1951) and legendary PONG (1972), right up to contemporary classics like Tomb Raider. There are plenty of opportunities to punch keyboards and waggle joysticks – and even get a jolly old electric shock via the two-player "Pain Station".

Boxhagener Platz market

MAP PAGE 92, POCKET MAP A17
Boxhagener Platz Ⓤ Samariterstr.

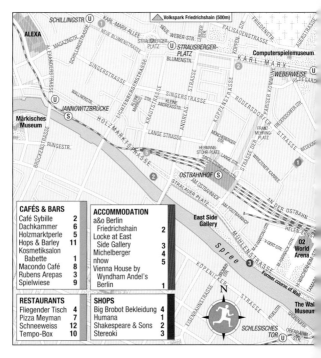

CAFÉS & BARS
Café Sybille	2
Dachkammer	6
Holzmarktperle	5
Hops & Barley	11
Kosmetiksalon Babette	1
Macondo Café	8
Rubens Arepas	3
Spielwiese	9

RESTAURANTS
Fliegender Tisch	4
Pizza Meyman	7
Schneeweiss	12
Tempo-Box	10

ACCOMMODATION
a&o Berlin Friedrichshain	2
Locke at East Side Gallery	3
Michelberger	4
nhow	5
Vienna House by Wyndham Andel's Berlin	1

SHOPS
Big Brobot Bekleidung	4
Humana	1
Shakespeare & Sons	2
Stereoki	3

ⓦ boxhagenerplatz.org. Farmers' market
Sat, flea market Sun.

The **Sunday flea market** at
Boxhagener Platz is a popular place
for locals and tourists alike. While
not as large as Mauerpark (see page
76), you can find vinyl, vintage
fashion, old crockery and more.

Oberbaumbrücke

MAP PAGE 92, POCKET MAP M7
ⓤ Warschauer Str.

This attractive, Spree-spanning
landmark connects the districts
of Friedrichshain and Kreuzberg,
today officially part of the same
borough but previously divided by
the Berlin Wall. The double-decker
bridge (and its name) dates back
to the eighteenth century when it
was originally constructed – from
wood – and acted as a gateway to
the city. A new version opened in
1896, designed by architect Otto
Stahn in brick gothic style. In 1945
the bridge was partly destroyed by

Oberbaumbrücke

the Wehrmacht to stop the Red
Army crossing it, and afterwards
ended up straddling the American

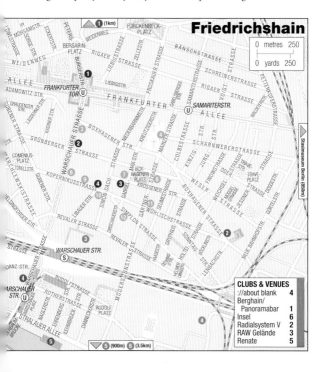

Stasi Museum

and Soviet sectors. When the Berlin Wall went up in 1961, the bridge became part of East Berlin's border with West Berlin; when it fell in 1989, the bridge was restored to its former appearance with a new steel middle section designed by Spanish architect Santiago Calatrava. Today the bridge stands as a symbol of unity between Friedrichshain and Kreuzberg (and is the site of a friendly "water battle" in summer). Look out for the neon *Stone Paper Scissors* installation by Thorsten Goldberg – a political statement about the arbitrariness of decisions to grant immigration or asylum status.

Stasi Museum

MAP PAGE 92, POCKET MAP M5
Ruschestr. 103, Haus 1, Lichtenberg
Ⓤ **Magdalenenstr.** Ⓦ **stasimuseum.de.**
Public tours every Mon, Wed, Fri & Sat
(English tours start 3pm).
East Germany's State Security Service – Stasi – struck terror into East Germans, using dark and duplicitous spying methods to unveil any potential signs of rebellion. This museum – in Lichtenberg, just east of Friedrichshain – used to be the **Stasi headquarters**: it was stormed and taken over when the Wall fell by an indignant group of people, many of whose lives had been affected by years of abuse, and members of this group still run the museum today. Following extensive renovations, the main building of the campus (Haus 1, which housed the Minister of State Security among others) reopened in 2012 and the exhibition "State Security in the SED Dictatorship" has been on permanent display since 2015. Visitors can see Stasi chief Erich Mielke's ridiculously immense desk (and equally large number of telephones) and the complex filing system that includes samples of body odours.

Shops

Big Brobot Bekleidung

MAP PAGE 92, POCKET MAP A16
Kopernikusstr. 19 ⓊⓈ Warschauerstr.
Ⓦ bigbrobot.net.
Friendly and vaguely trashy store
where you can browse rare toys, art
books and clothing.

Humana

MAP PAGE 92, POCKET MAP A16
Frankfurter Tor 3 Ⓤ Frankfurter Tor
Ⓦ humana-second-hand.de.
This immense five-storey
warehouse, part of a grand Soviet
"worker palace", brims with
secondhand clothes. The top floor
has the best vintage gear. Multiple
(smaller) branches across the city.

Shakespeare & Sons

MAP PAGE 92, POCKET MAP A16
Warschauerstr. 74 ⓊⓈ Warschauerstr.
Ⓦ shakespeareandsons.com.
One of the city's best English-
language bookshops, this is a
welcoming space filled with literary,
sci-fi and academic classics, as well
as a great selection of kids' books,
French-language titles and Berlin-
themed tomes. Inside, *Fine Bagels*
serves up some of the best bagels
in town.

Stereoki

MAP PAGE 92, POCKET MAP A17
Gabriel-Max-Str. 18 ⓊⓈ Warschauerstr.
Ⓦ stereoki.com.
This slick, white-walled men's
fashion store carries shoes,
trainers, wallets, bags, hats, tees
and more by brands like Adidas
and New Balance, Herschel
Supply and Element Emerald
Collection.

Restaurants

Fliegender Tisch

MAP PAGE 92, POCKET MAP B16
Mainzer Str. 10 Ⓤ Samariterstr.
Ⓦ fliegender-tisch.de.

Humana

"The flying table" is a small, cosy
place with just a few wooden
tables. It's justly popular thanks to
tasty Italian staples like thin-crust
pizza and risotto for decent prices.
€€

Pizza Meyman

MAP PAGE 92, POCKET MAP A17
Warschauer Str. 80 Ⓤ Frankfurter Tor
Ⓦ pizzeria-meyman.de.
This unassuming restaurant is
great for late-night cravings or
for a break between bar hops.
Ingredients are fresh, prices are
reasonable and there's usually a
table free. Pasta dishes and salads as
well as pizza. €

Schneeweiss

MAP PAGE 92, POCKET MAP A17
Simplonstr. 16 Ⓤ Warschauer Str.
Ⓦ schneeweiss-berlin.de.
One of Friedrichshain's few
upmarket restaurants, "Snow
White" is an understated place
with a minimalist design and a
menu that it describes as "Alpine" –
Italian, Austrian and south German
recipes such as Schnitzel and pasta.
There's a decent weekend brunch
(10am–3pm), a fireplace lounge

and a low-key bar vibe come evening. €€€

Tempo-Box

MAP PAGE 92, POCKET MAP A16
Simon-Dach Str. 15–16 ⑤ Warschauer Str.
ⓦ tempo-box.de.

This modern restaurant serves everything from eggy breakfasts to Argentinian rump steak, all set in the middle of Friedrichshain – during summer times you can enjoy watching the streets of Berlin from their sunny terrace. Make sure to get in before the daily Happy Hour (5–8pm) is over, as there over 160 cocktails to choose from. €€

Cafés and bars

Café Sybille

MAP PAGE 92, POCKET MAP L5
Karl-Marx-Allee 72 ⓤ Strausberger Platz
ⓦ cafe-sybille.org.

It's worth a stop at *Café Sybille* not just for the ice cream, cakes

and coffee, but because it also hosts a small museum about the history of Karl-Marx-Allee, with propaganda posters, socialist statues and other exhibits to browse while your drinks are made. The restaurant closed in 2018, which led to many upset Berliners. Luckily, a new owner was found and the café reopened its doors in 2019. €

Dachkammer

MAP PAGE 92, POCKET MAP A17
Simon-Dach-Str. 39 ⑤/ⓤ Warschauerstr.
ⓦ dachkammer.com.

The largest and possibly most sociable place on the strip – the combination of rustic bar downstairs and retro bar upstairs has made this a local classic.

Holzmarktperle

MAP PAGE 92, POCKET MAP J5
Holzmarktstr. 25 ⑤ Ostbahnhof
ⓦ holzmarkt.com.

House-roasted coffee at the café of the cooperative-run Holzmarkt

Berghain/Panoramabar

Café Sybille

25 creative quarter. The sprawling site on the Spree is also home to a beer garden, bakery, club, theatre and more.

Hops & Barley

MAP PAGE 92, POCKET MAP A17
Wühlischstr. 22/23 ⓤ Samariterstr. or ⓈⓤWarschauerstr. ⓦhopsandbarley-berlin.de.
This unassuming wood-and-tiles brewpub attracts a diverse crowd that ranges from international hipsters to elderly locals. Five draft beers (three standard and two experimental ones) that are produced on-site, supplemented by simple snacks such as sausages and brewer's grain bread.

Kosmetiksalon Babette

MAP PAGE 92, POCKET MAP K4
Karl-Marx-Allee 36 ⓤ Schillingstr. ⓦcafemoskau.com/salon-babette.
This glass box, once a GDR cosmetics shop, is now a chic and lively bar. At night, the only identifying marker is the warm glow of the cube's interior lights. The ground floor is sparsely furnished, while the former treatment rooms upstairs

occasionally have book readings and performances.

Macondo Café

MAP PAGE 92, POCKET MAP A17
Gärtnerstr. 14 ⓤ Samariterstr. ⓦmacondocafebar.com.
Kitted out with fraying vintage furniture, this local chill-out spot offers a good selection of books and board games and a great atmosphere for lounging. Good quality South American eats, too. €€

Rubens Arepas

MAP PAGE 92, POCKET MAP A16
Warschauer Str. 81 ⓤ Samariterstrasse ⓣ030 45 96 45 84.
Venezuelan street food place for a quick-sit lunch or on-the-go munch. As well as the titular arepa, order the cachapa. Good veggie and vegan options – and naturally gluten-free to boot. €

Spielwiese

MAP PAGE 92, POCKET MAP A17
Kopernikusstr. 24 ⓤ Warschauer Str. ⓦteam-spielwiese.de.
This café and games publisher stocks over 1800 games, from chess

Big Brobot

to Risk. For a small fee, you can play games in the café or rent them to take home.

Clubs and venues

://about blank

MAP PAGE 92, POCKET MAP M7
Markgrafendamm 24c ⓤ Ostkreuz
ⓦ aboutparty.net.

Set inside a nondescript concrete block, this is one of the city's better underground clubs, with two main dancefloors, lots of nooks and crannies, and a garden where DJs spin in the summer. The dominant music policy is house and techno with occasional forays into related electronic genres plus live concerts.

Berghain/Panoramabar

MAP PAGE 92, POCKET MAP L6
Am Wriezener Bahnhof ⓢ Ostbahnhof
ⓦ berghain.de.

A strong contender for best club in the city, if not the world, this former power station attracts techno fans from all over the globe for its fantastic sound system, purist music policy and awe-inspiring industrial interior. The best time to arrive is after 5am on Saturday morning; the club runs till Sunday evening. Famously, entry is very much not guaranteed – the club's door policy is notoriously unpredictable and whim-based. In 2017, the club opened up the ground floor for more experimental sounds.

Insel

MAP PAGE 92, POCKET MAP M7
Alt-Treptow 6, Treptow ⓢ Plänterwald
ⓦ inselberlin.de.

A reliable venue for thrash/punk gigs and club nights, on a Spree island that's part of Treptower Park. There are occasional outdoor raves on the large open terrace in summer.

Radialsystem V

MAP PAGE 92, POCKET MAP K6
Holzmarktstr. 33 ⓢ Ostbahnhof
ⓦ radialsystem.de.

This sprawling space, housed in a former pumping station on the Spree, was retrofitted and reopened as a space for the arts in 2006, with a glass extension added. As well as visual and performing arts exhibitions, it hosts events ranging from opera concerts to more relaxed jam sessions.

RAW Gelände

MAP PAGE 92, POCKET MAP A17
Revaler Str. 99 Ⓢ/Ⓤ Warschauerstr.
Ⓦ rawcc.org.

Sprawling, heavily graffitied ensemble of former train yard buildings, now one of the city's most alternative clubbing and cultural complexes. There are several shabby-chic bars and clubs, including the laidback Crack Bellmer (Ⓦ crackbellmer. de) and the more upbeat electro and techno clubs Cassiopeia (Ⓦ cassiopeia-berlin.de) and Lokschuppen (Ⓦ lokschuppen-

berlin.com). Urban Spree (Ⓦ urbanspree.com), a beer garden that often has DJs and live music late into the night, is at the Warschauer Strasse side, and there's even a chic outdoor swimming pool with a club and concert space called Haubentauscher (Ⓦ haubentaucher.berlin).

Renate

MAP PAGE 92, POCKET MAP M7
Alt-Stralau 70 Ⓢ Treptower Park.
Ⓦ renate.cc.

Located near the train tracks that run towards Treptower Park, *Renate* is an artist-run event space in a semi-derelict house with three floors, a cocktail bar and flamboyant decor that changes with each party. The music is good and the crowd is mixed. Sister club, *Else*, just across the bridge, hosts open-air parties and has a beer garden open from Wed–Sun.

Radialsystem V

West Kreuzberg

The western section of Kreuzberg is centred on the main streets of Gneisenaustrasse and Bergmannstrasse, and pretty Viktoriapark. Once one of the poorest areas in Berlin, it's now one of its most bourgeois and bohemian and lies in sharp contrast to the more scruffy, multicultural part of the district to the east. Indeed, walking along café- and boutique-lined streets like Bergmannstrasse you're reminded of the gentrified environs of Prenzlauer Berg. At the end of this street is Viktoriapark, whose Iron Cross monument gives the district its name, and nearby is Chamissoplatz, which hosts a popular organic farmers' market every Saturday morning.

Mauermuseum – Museum Haus am Checkpoint Charlie

MAP PAGE 102, POCKET MAP C15
Friedrichstr. 43–45 Ⓤ Kochstr.
Ⓦ mauermuseum.de. Charge.
"Checkpoint C" (or **"Checkpoint Charlie"** as it was called by the Western Allies) was the best-known Berlin Wall crossing point between East and West Berlin during the Cold War. Today it's one of the key places to learn about life in Berlin during the division. The museum – founded in 1962 by Dr Rainer Hildebrandt – is marked by the well-known "YOU ARE NOW LEAVING THE AMERICAN SECTOR" sign that remains outside the building alongside

Checkpoint Charlie

stone-faced (mock) guards and a replica of the checkpoint (the original is in the Allied Museum in Dahlem). One of the most visited museums in Berlin, its exhibitions focus mostly on the creative ways East Berliners tried to escape – hot-air balloons, vehicles with special compartments, even a one-man submarine. There are also exhibits on the concept of freedom and nonviolent protest in general, including the Charter 77 typewriter and Mahatma Gandhi's diary.

Topography of Terror

MAP PAGE 102, POCKET MAP F6
Niederkirchnerstr. 8 Ⓤ/Ⓢ Potsdamer Platz Ⓦ topographie.de. Free.

From 1933–1945, the headquarters of the **Gestapo**, their "house prison" and the Reich Security main office stood on this site, making it one of the most notorious locations of Nazi brutality. It's now called the Topography of Terror (Topographie des Terrors) documentation centre, and though many of the buildings were destroyed in World War II, visitors can walk around the largely open-air museum, where exhibits display the history of the site, and explore the events of the Holocaust. A documentation centre focuses on the central institutions of the SS and police in the Third Reich and their crimes. The displays are graphic, so families with children should exercise caution. An audio guide is available.

Martin-Gropius-Bau

MAP PAGE 102, POCKET MAP F6
Niederkirchnerstr. 7 Ⓤ/Ⓢ Potsdamer Platz Ⓦ gropiusbau.de. Charge.

Envisioned as an applied arts museum, the stunning Martin-Gropius-Bau has evolved into one of Berlin's major contemporary art venues. The ornate, Renaissance-style building was badly damaged during World War II, and rebuilt 1978–81. It draws big-name international displays on art and history, such as

Deutsches Technikmuseum

retrospectives of Frida Kahlo and Méret Oppenheim and exhibitions by the likes of Ai Weiwei.

Anhalter Bahnhof

MAP PAGE 102, POCKET MAP F7
Askanischer Platz 6 Ⓤ Mendelssohn-Bartholdy-Park Ⓣ 030 50 58 68 30. Free.

This haunting landmark is a remnant of the Anhalter Bahnhof, once one of Berlin's busiest railway stations. The terminus opened in 1841, but its notoriety stems from World War II when it was one of the three stations used to deport Jews to Theresienstadt (or Terezín), and from there to the death camps. Nearly ten thousand Jews were deported from here, usually in groups of fifty to a hundred; the last train left on March 27, 1945. Though badly damaged in World War II, it was only closed in 1952. Today, all that remains is a portion of the entrance facade and a commemorative plaque, though an S-Bahn station shares its name.

Deutsches Technikmuseum

MAP PAGE 102, POCKET MAP F7
Trebbiner Str. 9 Ⓤ Gleisdreieck Ⓦ www.

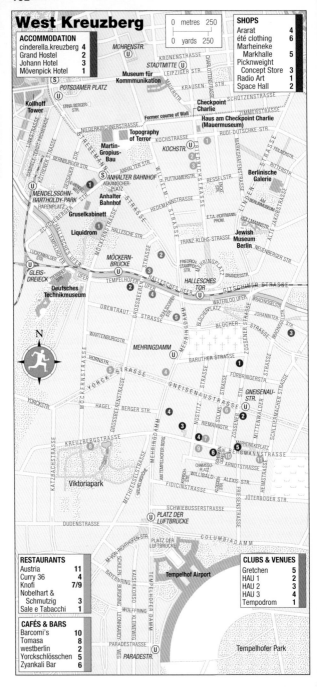

West Kreuzberg

0 metres 250

0 yards 250

ACCOMMODATION

cinderella.kreuzberg	4
Grand Hostel	2
Johann Hotel	3
Mövenpick Hotel	1

SHOPS

Ararat	4
été clothing	6
Marheineke Markhalle	5
Picknweight Concept Store	3
Radio Art	1
Space Hall	2

RESTAURANTS

Austria	11
Curry 36	4
Knofi	7/9
Nobelhart & Schmutzig	3
Sale e Tabacchi	1

CAFÉS & BARS

Barcomi's	10
Tomasa	8
westberlin	2
Yorckschlösschen	5
Zyankali Bar	6

CLUBS & VENUES

Gretchen	5
HAU 1	2
HAU 2	3
HAU 3	4
Tempodrom	1

sdtb.de. Charge.

Opened in 1982 in the former goods depot of the Anhalter Bahnhof, the German Technology Museum presents a comprehensive (some might say overwhelming) overview of German technology. The vast collection includes trains, planes, computers, radios, cameras and more. There's a strong emphasis on rail, with trains from 1835 to the present day, but there are also maritime and aviation halls and exhibits on the Industrial Revolution, the computer and space age, and the pharmaceutical and chemical industry. A new exhibition on information and communication networks and the history of mobility is housed in the annexe on Ladestrasse. Much of the museum is based on life-sized reproductions and actual machines, though the Science Center Spectrum annexe at Möckernstrasse 26 is more interactive.

Jewish Museum Berlin

MAP PAGE 102, POCKET MAP G7
Lindenstr. 9–14 ⓤ Hallesches Tor/Kochstr.
ⓦ www.jmberlin.de. Free; charge for temporary exhibitions.

Daniel Libeskind's Jewish Museum (Jüdisches Museum) is a must-see, both historically and architecturally. The stark, zinc-covered building has been thoughtfully designed, with each element symbolizing various aspects of the historical Jewish experience over some two thousand years. The process of moving through the building – which really is a work of art – is an experience in itself, not least thanks to its five vertical voids and walls of dark concrete. **Guided tours** are available and the **restaurant** serving traditional Jewish cuisine (though not kosher) is very good.

Berlinische Galerie

MAP PAGE 102, POCKET MAP H7
Alte Jakobstr. 124–128 ⓤ Hallesches Tor/
Kochstr. ⓦ berlinischegalerie.de. Guided tours in English first Mon of month at 3pm.

The Memory Void, Jewish Museum Berlin

Charge.

Founded in 1975 as a private institution, the Berlinische Galerie was once part of the Martin-Gropius-Bau before moving to its current premises in 2004. Its mission is to showcase art made in Berlin, bringing together fine art, photography and architecture. The permanent exhibition includes works from 1870 to the present day, spanning major movements such as the Secessionists, Fluxus, Dada and the Expressionists, with works by Max Liebermann, Otto Dix, Georg Grosz and Hannah Höch. A spacious hall also hosts temporary exhibitions and there are tours, occasional lectures and film screenings.

Berlin Story Museum & Hitler Documentation

MAP PAGE 102, POCKET MAP F7
Schöneberger Str. 23a ⓤ Mendelssohn-
Bartholdy-Park ⓦ berlinstory.de. Charge.

This attraction, set inside a WW2 bunker, features 800 years of Berlin history (free audio guide included) in the Berlin Story Museum, plus a more controversial exhibition about Adolf Hitler's life and WW2

Tempelhofer Park

that includes a reconstruction of his living and working rooms from the original "Führerbunker" near Potsdamer Platz.

Viktoriapark

MAP PAGE 102, POCKET MAP F9
Between Kreuzbergstr, Dudenstr, Katzbachstr. and Methfesselstr. Ⓤ Yorckstr/ Mehringdamm.

Famous for hosting Berlin's highest peak, "Vikky Park" is one of the most popular in the city. A multitude of pathways winds around and up the hill to give visitors stunning panoramic views, and there are playgrounds, landscaped rose gardens, a tumbling waterfall and even vineyards to enjoy and explore; the well-known *Golgatha* **beer garden** provides shade and sustenance.

Tempelhofer Park

MAP PAGE 102, POCKET MAP G9
Columbiadamm 192 Ⓤ Südstern
Ⓦ tempelhofer-park.de. Free. Airport tours (2hr; English language) Charge. Booking: Ⓦ thf-berlin.de.

The largest park in continental Europe, Tempelhofer Park is the site of the now **defunct Tempelhof airport**, an immense building created by the Nazis (the terminal was designed to resemble an eagle) which became famous for the 1948–49 Berlin Airlift. **Tours** of the airport building, which stages events through the year, relate the story. The huge space surrounding the airport doesn't boast any actual attractions but is still a great place to go cycling, walking, roller-skating – or to enjoy a picnic (which can be purchased on site).

Liquidrom

MAP PAGE 102, POCKET MAP F7
Möckernstr. 10 Ⓤ Möckernbrücke
Ⓦ liquidrom-berlin.de.

This designer **spa** features saunas, slightly cramped chill-out areas and a large, domed flotation pool where you can drift and listen to soft electronic music, sometimes mixed live by DJs, as well as readings and live concerts. A range of massage treatments are also available.

Shops

Ararat

MAP PAGE 102, POCKET MAP G9
Bergmannstr. 99a Ⓤ Gneisenaustr.
Ⓦ ararat-berlin.de.

It's easy to lose yourself in here, surrounded by prints and picture frames, postcards and gifts.

été clothing

MAP PAGE 102, POCKET MAP G9
Bergmannstr. 18 Ⓤ Gneisenaustr. Ⓦ ete-clothing.de.

With shirts and hoodies from trusted brands like RVLT, Volcom and Iriedaily, and a decent range of sneakers, this is a good stop for contemporary wear in Kreuzberg.

Marheineke Markhalle

MAP PAGE 102, POCKET MAP G9
Marheinekeplatz 15 Ⓤ Gneisenaustr.
Ⓦ meine-markthalle.de.

This popular covered market hall is an excellent place for grocery shopping as well as for breakfasts and lunches. Stalls often emphasize organic and regional products. You'll also find crêpes and tapas, as well as regular art exhibitions and events.

Picknweight Concept Store

MAP PAGE 102, POCKET MAP G9
Bergmannstr. 102 Ⓤ Mehringdamm
Ⓦ picknweight.de.

By-the-kilo retro paradise with secondhand clothes spanning the 1960s to 1990s – particularly good on the 1970s.

Radio Art

MAP PAGE 102, POCKET MAP G8
Zossener Str. 2 Ⓤ Mehringdamm Ⓦ radio-art.de.

A visually satisfying shop for radio lovers, its shelves brimming with vintage (and some modern) radio sets and record players.

Space Hall

MAP PAGE 102, POCKET MAP G8
Zossener Str. 35 Ⓤ Gneisenaustr.
Ⓦ spacehall.de.

This excellent record shop offers a large CD collection (rock, pop, electronic, rap) and masses of vinyl.

Radio Art

WEST KREUZBERG

Restaurants

Austria

MAP PAGE 102, POCKET MAP G9
Bergmannstr. 30, on Marheineke Platz
Ⓤ Gneisenaustr. ⓦ austria-berlin.de.
Austria serves classic Austrian
dishes, using organic ingredients, in
a hunting lodge-style interior. The
huge Schnitzel is justly famous. €€€

Curry 36

MAP PAGE 102, POCKET MAP G8
Mehringdamm 36 Ⓤ Mehringdamm
ⓦ curry36.de.
Everyone in Berlin has a favourite
place to eat *Currywurst* – sausage
doused in curry ketchup – but
Curry 36 is cited more often than
most (along with *Konnopke's*, see
page 84); its popularity alone
guarantees it's a buzzy place to grab
a snack. €

Knofi

MAP PAGE 102, POCKET MAP G9
Bergmannstr. 98 Ⓤ Gneisenaustr. ⓦ knofi.de
A small deli-style restaurant serving
tasty Turkish food. Breakfast plates,

cigar-shaped borek and homemade
lentil soup are favourites, but the
manti (Turkish ravioli, available
veggie or non-veggie) is the
speciality here. €

Nobelhart & Schmutzig

MAP PAGE 102, POCKET MAP G6
Friedrichstr. 218 Ⓤ Kochstr./Checkpoint
Charlie ⓦ nobelhartundschmutzig.com.
Founded by sommelier Billy
Wagner, formerly of *Weinbar Rutz*
(see page 35), and chef Micha
Schäfer, this chic spot offers
delicious, creative food, fiercely
committed to a local and seasonal
ethos. €€€€

Sale e Tabacchi

MAP PAGE 102, POCKET MAP G6
Rudi-Dutschke-Str. 23 Ⓤ Kochstr. ⓦ sale-
e-tabacchi.de.
Located towards the Mitte end
of Kreuzberg, "Salt and Tobacco"
has a more classic feel than most
restaurants in the area. It's known
for its excellent seafood dishes and
Italian wines; the menu changes
daily. The interior is large and airy
and there's a garden out back. €€€

Tempodrom

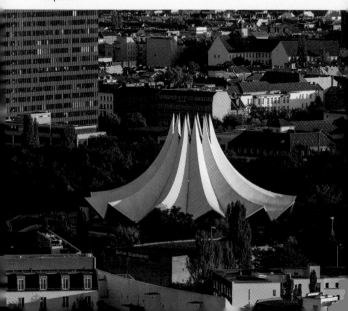

Cafés and bars

Barcomi's

MAP PAGE 102, POCKET MAP G9
Bergmannstr. 21 Ⓤ Gneisenaustr.
Ⓦ barcomis.de.

You can find excellent quality coffee at this cosey spot– Barcomi's roasts its twelve coffee varieties here, hence the decorative coffee sacks and delicious smell – as well as handmade breads, pastries, soups and sandwiches. They also large occasion cakes for pre-order. €

Tomasa

MAP PAGE 102, POCKET MAP F9
Kreuzbergstr. 62 Ⓤ Mehringdamm
Ⓦ tomasa.de.

This old-school villa, on the edge of Viktoriapark, is a particularly pleasant place for a relaxed breakfast or lunch. The classic interior, good seasonal menu (from tapas to pasta and German dishes) and friendly service attract a mixed clientele, families included. Sunday brunch is very popular. €€

westberlin

MAP PAGE 102, POCKET MAP G6
Alexandrinenstr. 118-121 Ⓤ Kochstr.
Ⓦ westberlin-bar-shop.de.

This handsome haven is part chic media hangout and part café; you can sip on a locally roasted flat white while working away on your laptop or enjoying a delicious cake, sandwich or quiche. They also have a decent selection of fashion and style magazines.

Yorckschlösschen

MAP PAGE 102, POCKET MAP F8
Yorckstr. 15 Ⓤ Mehringdamm
Ⓦ yorckschloesschen.de.

This place has been a Kreuzberg institution for over a hundred years, though it doesn't seem to have been updated since the 1970s. The menu is mostly basic and local – meatballs and Leberkäse (meatloaf) – and the service gruff, but the tree-shaded garden is a very pleasant place to eat. Live jazz, blues and country bands play most days.

Zyankali Bar

MAP PAGE 102, POCKET MAP G8
Gneisenaustr. 17 Ⓤ Gneisenaustr.
Ⓦ zyankali.de.

This unique "herbal clinic" bar has an incredible range of strange and surprising cocktails (often with homemade ingredients), occasional DJs, a "play area" with football and pinball and a beer garden with plenty of seating. Alcohol-infused ice cream (summer only) and snacks like dim sum and Hawaiian toast are also served.

Clubs and venues

Gretchen

MAP PAGE 102, POCKET MAP G8
Obentrautstr. 19-21 Ⓤ Hallesches Tor
Ⓦ gretchen-club.de.

Named after a murderous character in Goethe's Faust, this alternative club space offers a handsome interior that's all columns and vaulted ceilings, and a mix of electronic sounds (drum 'n' bass, dubstep, trip hop). A refreshing alternative to the usual Berlin "techno-shack" formula.

Hebbel am Ufer

MAP PAGE 102, POCKET MAP G7
HAU1 Stresemannstr. 29; HAU2 Hallesches Ufer 32; HAU3 Tempelhofer Ufer 10
Ⓤ Hallesches Tor Ⓦ hebbel-am-ufer.de.

These three neighbouring venues of HAU Hebbel am Ufer – HAU1, HAU2 and HAU3 – are the places for ground-breaking theatre, the occasional concert and more.

Tempodrom

MAP PAGE 102, POCKET MAP F7
Möckernstr. 10 Ⓤ Möckernbrücke
Ⓦ tempodrom.de.

A giant tent-like arena in the heart of Berlin, Tempodrom puts on concerts, shows, plays, galas, conferences, fashion shows – you name it, Tempodrom's hosted it.

East Kreuzberg

An isolated section of West Berlin throughout the Cold War, Kreuzberg has since grown into one of Berlin's most colourful districts – a magnet for left-wing anarchists, LGBTQIA+ culture, Turkish immigrants (it's sometimes called Little Istanbul) and, increasingly, hipsters and tourists. Despite being a coherent borough (nowadays part of Kreuzberg-Friedrichshain), Kreuzberg is still largely considered two distinct halves roughly coterminous with their former postal codes: SO 36 and SW 61 in the eastern and western sides respectively. Much of the eastern part of Kreuzberg abutted the wall on the West side and was strongly associated with Berlin's squatter and anarchist scenes. Though the area has gentrified somewhat since those heady days, it maintains a grungy, vibrant feel that spreads out from Schlesisches Tor down to Kottbusser Tor and beyond, fuelled by an ever-expanding series of excellent independent bars, clubs and restaurants.

East Kreuzberg

FOOD MARKET	
Markthalle Neun	3

RESTAURANTS	
Baraka	10
Cocolo	18
Defne	16
Kimchi Princess	12
Long March Canteen	1
Ma-Makan	7
Maroush	6
Musashi	17
Taka Fish House	11

CAFÉS & BARS	
Ankerklause	15
Burgermeister	4
Club der Visionaere	14
Five Elephant	19
Möbel-Olfe	9
Roses	8
Tiki Heart	13
Schwarze Traube	2
Würgeengel	5

FHXB Friedrichshain-Kreuzberg Museum

MAP PAGE 108, POCKET MAP J7
Adalbertstr. 95A ⓤ Kottbusser Tor ⓦ fhxb-museum.de. Free.

Chronicling the history of two of Berlin's most vibrant districts – Friedrichshain and Kreuzberg – this small but fascinating museum features permanent exhibitions (in English and German) covering important social issues in the area, covering topics such as urban development, gentrification and immigration. There's also a fascinating calendar of temporary exhibitions; check online before visiting. The museum also hosts the **Gerd Schneider Museum Printing Shop**, which features an original 1928 printing press and offers a range of **workshops** for kids where they can learn different printing techniques such as linocut, woodcut, etching, screen printing and typographic hand typesetting.

Kunstraum Kreuzberg/Bethanien

MAP PAGE 108, POCKET MAP K7
Mariannenpl. 2 ⓤ Kottbusser Tor ⓦ kunstraumkreuzberg.de. Free.

Located in a **former hospital**, the *Bethanien* is now a contemporary **art and music studio space** that hosts a lively calendar of temporary exhibitions, workshops, films, artists' talks and walking tours. In the 1970s, squatting and various citizen initiatives saved this historical building from the brink of demolition, and since then, its grand halls have been a creative and cultural hub for the community. The building itself is worth the visit alone; built in 1847, it is impressive in size with ornate arches and a grand entrance hall. There's also a rather striking **café** and **restaurant** in the hospital's vaulted hall, which opens onto a Biergarten in the summer. They also host outdoor cinema screening too.

EAST KREUZBERG

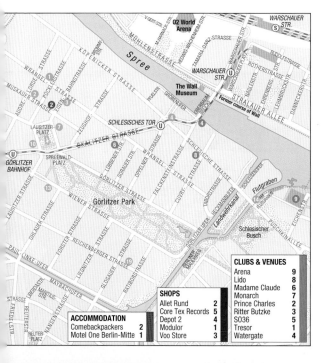

SHOPS

Allet Rund	2
Core Tex Records	5
Depot 2	4
Modulor	1
Voo Store	3

CLUBS & VENUES

Arena	9
Lido	8
Madame Claude	6
Monarch	7
Prince Charles	2
Ritter Butzke	3
SO36	5
Tresor	1
Watergate	4

ACCOMMODATION

Comebackpackers	2
Motel One Berlin-Mitte	1

Shops

Allet Rund

MAP PAGE 108, POCKET MAP J7
Dresdener Str. 16 Ⓤ Kottbusser Tor
Ⓦ alletrund.de.

Joachin Semrau offers fairtrade, Kreuzberg-made designs for sizes 42 to 60, using European fabrics.

Core Tex Records

MAP PAGE 108, POCKET MAP K7
Oranienstr. 3 Ⓤ Görlitzer Bahnhof
Ⓦ coretexrecords.com.

The best place for punk and hardcore music, plus T-shirts, accessories, books and concert tickets.

Depot 2

MAP PAGE 108, POCKET MAP K7
Oranienstr. 9 Ⓤ Görlitzer Bahnhof
Ⓦ depot2.de.

An ice-cool assortment of street-oriented fashions, including Vans and other stylish footwear.

Modulor

MAP PAGE 108, POCKET MAP J7

Core Tex Records

Prinzenstr. 85 Ⓤ Moritzplatz Ⓦ modulor.de.
Two floors and 3,000 m² of supplies for designers, artists and architects, professional or otherwise. An institution and a treasure trove for adults and children, worthy of an almighty browse.

Voo Store

MAP PAGE 108, POCKET MAP J7
Oranienstr. 24 Ⓤ Kottbusser Tor
Ⓦ voostore.com.

A former locksmiths turned pop-culture concept shop, Voo Store's gorgeous interior was created by Danish designer and architect Sigurd Larsen, while its highly curated stock features both big names and little-known designers.

Food market

Markthalle Neun

MAP PAGE 108, POCKET MAP K7
Eisenbahnstr. 42/43 Ⓤ Görlitzer Bahnhof
Ⓦ markthalleneun.com. Basic market Tues–Thurs; farmers' market Fri & Sat; shops Mon–Sat.

This revitalized nineteenth-century market hall has become Berlin's foodie destination, thanks to a weekly farmers' market (Fri & Sat), events focusing on sustainable and local produce and the especially popular weekly Street Food Thursday event.

Restaurants

Baraka

MAP PAGE 108, POCKET MAP K7
Lausitzer Platz 6 Ⓤ Görlitzer Bahnhof
Ⓦ restaurant-baraka.eatbu.com.

North African food fans will adore *Baraka*. The decor is authentic without slipping into kitsch (although the back room comes close) and the food – *tagines*, chicken skewers, *schwarma* – is some of the best in town, and at decent prices. The mixed plates for two are immense. €

Cocolo

MAP PAGE 108, POCKET MAP K8
Graefestr. 11 Ⓤ Kottbusser Tor Ⓦ kuchi.de/
restaurant/cocolo-x-berg.

One of Berlin's best dedicated *ramen* spot, *Cocolo* started life with its Mitte branch (Gipstr. 3) before expanding to Kreuzberg in 2014. Slurp your way through their short menu of soups and snacks (including sweet pork belly and *kimchi ramen*) at a shared table inside. €€

Defne

MAP PAGE 108, POCKET MAP J8
Planufer 92c Ⓤ Kottbusser Tor/
Schönleinstr. Ⓣ 030 81 79 71 11.

Defne's Turkish and Mediterranean classics include *imam bayildi* (aubergines with pine nuts, peppers and tomato sauce) and lamb skewers. The interior is simple and spacious; the terrace, overlooking the Landwehrkanal, is lovely in summer. €

Kimchi Princess

MAP PAGE 108, POCKET MAP K7

Skalitzer Str. 36 Ⓤ Kottbusser Tor
Ⓦ kimchiprincess.com.

Part of a trend for cool Korean eateries in Berlin, *Kimchi Princess* offers simple wooden pallets as seating, a spacious interior and hipster staff. There's *bibimbap* and more on the menu, but the Korean barbecue is the thing to go for. The owners also run the nearby *Angry Chicken* (Oranienstr. 16), a must for spice fans. €€€

Long March Canteen

MAP PAGE 108, POCKET MAP K7
Wrangelstr. 20 Ⓤ Görlitzer Bahnhof
Ⓦ longmarchcanteen.com.

Although folk justifiably flock here for the *dim sum*, this trendy Chinese restaurant also serves up excellent, tapas-sized portions of other dishes like *pak choi* salad and marinated chicken skewers with water chestnuts. John Malkovich is just one of the A-listers who has been spotted here. €€€€

Ma-Makan

MAP PAGE 108, POCKET MAP K7
Lausitzer Pl. 12 Ⓤ Görlitzer Bahnhof
Ⓦ mamakanberlin.com.

This Singaporean and Malaysian restaurant is worth the plentiful hype. The Hainanese chicken rice is particularly good, and the revolving specials menu offers up something new each time you walk through the door. It's a particularly good spot for brunch too – highlights include croissants filled with homemade pandan coconut custard and slathered in a salted coconut glaze. €€

Maroush

MAP PAGE 108, POCKET MAP J7
Adalbertstr. 93 Ⓤ Kottbusser Tor Ⓣ 030
69 53 61 71.

With a cosy dining area, Middle Eastern decor and tasty sandwiches, kebabs, falafels and fresh salads, this small Lebanese restaurant is one of the better of its type. Plenty of vegetarian options available. €

Musashi

MAP PAGE 108, POCKET MAP J8
Kottbusser Damm 102 Ⓤ Schönleinstr.
Ⓣ 030 69 32 042.

This tiny spot serves up decent sushi in a refreshingly designer-free space, decorated with posters of sumo wrestlers and populated with just a few bar tables. The Japanese chefs prepare fresh, tasty *makis* and inside-out rolls for very good prices. €

Taka Fish House

MAP PAGE 108, POCKET MAP J7
Adalbertstr. 97 Ⓤ Kottbusser Tor Ⓣ 0157 74 24 62 19.

Tucked away on bustling Kottbusser Tor and surrounded by kebab and falafel shops, this unassuming Turkish *Imbiss* has just a handful of tables inside and out but serves up some of the most delicious, freshly grilled fish sandwiches in the city. The sardine plate is a thing of beauty. €€

Cafés and bars

Ankerklause

MAP PAGE 108, POCKET MAP J8
Kottbusser Damm 104 Ⓤ Kottbusser Tor
Ⓦ ankerklause.de.

Situated by Maybachufer, next to the Turkish market (Tues & Fri; see page 117), *Ankerklause* is a popular café during the day, with a decent range of snacks (and seats out front and a terrace overlooking the water out back). Later, there's something of the alternative scene about it when the jukebox plays rock 'n' roll classics. €

Burgermeister

MAP PAGE 108, POCKET MAP L7
Oberbaumstrasse. 8 Ⓤ Schlesisches Tor
Ⓦ burgermeister.com.

Top spot for burgers in the city, located under the elevated tracks of the U1 at Schlesisches Tor in a former public toilet. Grab a seat outdoors or take your new favourite burger down to the

Spree. A Berlin burger success story, they've got outposts across the capital. €

Club der Visionaere

MAP PAGE 108, POCKET MAP M8
Am Flutgraben 1 Ⓤ Schlesisches Tor
Ⓦ clubdervisionaere.com.

Just beyond the Kreuzberg/Treptow border, this legendary summer-only techno bar enjoys a unique setting on the intersection of the Spree and Flutgraben canal. The bar and DJ booth is in an old ceramic-tiled boathouse, and punters stand (and dance) on the floating docks outside. It's minimal techno all the way and a fantastically upbeat place.

Five Elephant

MAP PAGE 108, POCKET MAP L8
Reichenberger Str. 101 Ⓤ Görlitzer Bahnhof
Ⓦ fiveelephant.com.

Opened by American and Austrian team Kris Shackman and Sophie Weigensamer in 2010, this highly regarded café not only brews (and roasts) some of the best "third wave" coffee in town, but it also has a much-talked-about cheesecake selection. There are more locations across town, including at Alte Schönhauser Str. 14, in Mitte, but this Kreuzberg outpost is the original. €

Möbel-Olfe

MAP PAGE 108, POCKET MAP J7
Reichenberger Str. 177 Ⓤ Kottbusser Tor
Ⓦ moebel-olfe.de.

Sandwiched between a string of Turkish snack bars in a run-down building behind Kottbusser Tor, this unusual, smoky, local bar attracts LGBTQIA+ folk, hipsters, ageing drunks and more. There are regular DJ nights, but it's more about experiencing the diversity of the Kreuzberg crowds.

Roses

MAP PAGE 108, POCKET MAP K7
Oranienstr. 187 Ⓤ Kottbusser Tor/Görlitzer Bahnhof Ⓣ 030 61 56 570.

Kimchi Princess

A legendary queer hangout, *Roses* provides a welcoming bosom for all manner of sexual orientations to crowd around. The kitsch decor mirrors the clientele and the fun vibe well. Sunday is the main day – and the most popular with gay men – but women are welcome anytime.

Schwarze Traube

MAP PAGE 108, POCKET MAP K7
Muskauer Str. 15 Ⓤ Görlitzer Bahnhof
Ⓣ 030 23 13 55 69.
Like many of Berlin's best drinking spots, this cocktail bar looks fairly nondescript from the outside. Knock on the door and – if it's not full – you'll be ushered into a cosy, dimly lit bar with rickety furnishings and award-winning drinks.

Tiki Heart

MAP PAGE 108, POCKET MAP K8
Wiener Str. 20 Ⓤ Görlitzer Bahnhof
Ⓦ tikiheart.de.
Berlin's only Hawaiian rockabilly-themed joint is renowned for its unapologetically kitsch interior and fun menu. The breakfasts, served

till 5pm, feature items like the "Oi-Fast" – a heady mix of scrambled eggs and chorizo. There are veggie burgers and – one for the serious rockers – a Lemmy burger grilled in whisky. Strong cocktails are served and the *Wild at Heart* club next door (Ⓦ wildatheartberlin.de) roars into action with regular rock, punk, metal and surf nights. €

Würgeengel

MAP PAGE 108, POCKET MAP J7
Dresdener Str. 122 Ⓤ Kottbusser Tor
Ⓦ wuergeengel.de.
One of the best cocktail bars in Kreuzberg, "the exterminating angel" has red walls, great tapas, decadent decor and an extensive cocktail and wine list. The feel is timeless, though with a trendy clientele.

Clubs and venues

Arena

MAP PAGE 108, POCKET MAP M8
Eichenstr. 4 Ⓤ Treptower Park Ⓦ arena-berlin.de.

This huge area next to the Spree encompasses the *Arena Club*, *Glashaus*, the actual Arena, the *Badeschiff* and the *Hoppetosse*. There are frequent electronic open-air parties and live acts at *Arena Club*, sometimes the *Hoppetosse* café (on a boat) can turn into a club, and at Arena itself you can catch rock and metal shows, as well as events and festivals.

Lido

MAP PAGE 108, POCKET MAP L7
Cuvrystr. 7 ⓤ Schlesisches Tor ⓦ lido-berlin.de.
An old-school club in a former theatre that's been going for a couple of decades, *Lido* is known for championing new music and is home to a younger indie crowd, with the occasional techno or house event. The club also has a courtyard with canopy that makes

it suitable for winter throw-downs.

Madame Claude

MAP PAGE 108, POCKET MAP L7
Lübbener Str. 19 ⓤ Görlitzer Bahnhof
ⓦ madameclaude.de.
This quirky hangout has live music six days a week, ranging from indie-rock and experimental to folk. Be prepared to feel slightly unsettled by the decor, which is upside down and hanging from the ceiling. Pay what you can for the entrance fee.

Monarch

MAP PAGE 108, POCKET MAP J7
Skalitzer Str. 134 ⓤ Kottbusser Tor
ⓦ kottimonarch.de.
Unpretentious and slightly ragged place that attracts a hip crowd who groove to a wide range of tunes – swing, rockabilly, folk,

punk, indie (no techno) – and enjoy views over Kottbusser Tor from huge windows. Entrance is via an unmarked door and stairwell next to Foto Kotti camera shop.

Prince Charles

MAP PAGE 108, POCKET MAP K7
Prinzenstr. 85f Ⓤ Moritzplatz Ⓦ princecharlesberlin.com.

Hidden away in a basement near Moritzplatz that once housed a swimming pool, this square-shaped, fairly upscale club has a penchant for bass-heavy parties that transcend techno tropes in favour of house, jazzy beats and hip-hop spun by a mix of local and international DJs.

Ritter Butzke

MAP PAGE 108, POCKET MAP H7
Ritter Str. 24 Ⓤ Moritzplatz Ⓦ club. ritterbutzke.com.

This former factory now comprises two main club rooms and an outside space, generally used only in summer. The music is usually electronic (house, electro, techno) and the crowd a considered but dedicated bunch.

SO36

MAP PAGE 108, POCKET MAP K7
Oranienstr. 190 Ⓤ Görlitzer Bahnhof Ⓦ so36.com.

One of the city's most legendary clubs, *SO36* has its roots in punk, post-punk and alternative music – musical heroes who've played here include Iggy Pop, David Bowie and Einstürzende Neubauten. Nowadays it hosts alternative and electronic shows, including monthly parties like Gayhane, a "QueerOriental" party, and "Ich bin ein Berliner", where you can catch an array of Berlin-based artists playing everything from garage to synth-pop.

Tresor

MAP PAGE 108, POCKET MAP J6
Köpenicker Str. 70 Ⓤ/Ⓢ Heinrich-Heine-

Roses

Str./Jannowitzbrücke. Ⓦ tresorberlin.com.

Housed in what used to be the main central-heating power station for East Berlin, the colossal location of the third incarnation of this ground-breaking club is breathtaking. Only a tiny portion of its 28,000 square metres is in use, but the club is still sizeable enough with three different rooms dedicated to cutting-edge, muscular techno played by a rotating roster of esteemed international (and local) DJs.

Watergate

MAP PAGE 108, POCKET MAP L7
Falckensteinstr. 49 Ⓤ Schlesisches Tor Ⓦ water-gate.de.

This slick, split-level club right on the Spree enjoys a killer combination of panoramic windows with epic river views, excellent sound systems and a constant flow of renowned international DJs. Music is electro, house and minimal techno. The crowd is fun and lively and usually pretty welcoming. However it can get really packed out on the weekends.

Neukölln

Neukölln, with its strings of bars, galleries, shops and cafés, is one of the city's most overtly hip districts. Once upon a time it was Rixdorf, a tiny village outside Berlin studded with windmills and boasting fantastic views from its impressive hillsides. In came the Industrial Revolution and away went the hills (used for buildings as the city expanded), and Rixdorf developed into a district of entertainment and revelry – so much so that in 1912 it was renamed Neukölln in an effort to change its riotous image. Postwar Neukölln became home to many Turkish, Arab and Kurdish communities, who still give the area its character, along with the more recent influx of expats and artists priced out of Berlin's other inner-city districts. Indeed, the resultant clash of working-class residents and middle-class creatives – reflected in intensely rising rents and the odd juxtapositions of gaudy video arcades and hipster hangouts around Weserstrasse and bustling Hermannplatz – forms the heart of Berlin's gentrification debate and lends Neukölln its somewhat edgy reputation.

Alt-Rixdorf

MAP PAGE 117
Ⓤ Karl-Marx-Str.

The most obvious reminders of Neukölln's medieval origins lie between the main arteries of Karl-Marx-Strasse and Sonnenallee, an area known as Alt-Rixdorf. A wander around the cobbled streets – centred on historical **Richardplatz** – reveals a centuries-old blacksmith's business, attractive churches and the remains of the district's eighteenth-century Bohemian village – founded for Protestant refugees fleeing persecution – with its cute houses and attractive gardens.

Körnerpark

MAP PAGE 117
Schierker Str. 8 Ⓢ Berlin-Neukölln
Ⓦ körnerpark.de. Free.

Refined Körnerpark might not be the biggest park in Neukölln, but it is easily the prettiest – a stark contrast to the vast, featureless expanse of nearby Tempelhofer Park (see page 104). With its manicured hedges, elegant promenades and marble fountains, it provides an ideal setting for wedding photos and summertime events such as galas, fairs and concerts. The charming, ivy-covered **Orangerie** – unique among Berlin's parks – is a highlight and contains the elegant *Orangerie Neukölln café*, which has a popular outdoor terrace in the warmer months.

Volkspark Hasenheide

MAP PAGE 117, POCKET MAP J9
Entrances on Hasenheide, Columbiadamm and Karlsgartenstr. Ⓤ Hermannplatz.
Open 24hr.

Originally used as a hunting ground for the Grand Elector in the seventeenth century, then as parade grounds for the Prussian military, this green expanse in the heart of Neukölln is today the domain of local sun-worshippers and picnickers. The long rows of trees are reminders of the former shooting ranges but little else of the park's past remains; instead, the main draws are a popular petting zoo, restaurant and a (summer-only) open-air stage for music, films and theatre. A popular funfair is also held in the southern part of the park each May.

Türkenmarkt

MAP PAGE 117, POCKET MAP K8
Maybachufer Str. Schönleinstr.
tuerkenmarkt.de. Tues & Fri.
Located on the border between Neukölln and Kreuzberg (Kreuzkölln as it's widely known), the twice-weekly Turkish Market has become an institution for Berlin's significant Turkish population as well as families, hipsters and tourists. It's colourfully chaotic, complete with yelling vendors peddling the usual arrays of fruit and vegetables, fabric and shoe stalls, stands selling tasty snacks and, occasionally, live music.

Ramones Museum

MAP PAGE 117, POCKET MAP L9
Weserstr. 159 Rathaus Neukölln
ramonesmuseum.com. Free.
Berlin's shrine to the American proto-punks, the Ramones Museum was started by music editor Flo Hayler more than two decades ago. Back then the collection amounted to a few signed posters and some T-shirts, but today it has expanded to over a thousand items of memorabilia. It's certainly an eclectic assortment, ranging from childhood photos of the group to gig set lists and flyers. In new digs in Neukölln after twenty years in Kreuzberg, the museum is displayed in a vegan diner and bar called 19:77, selling coffee, beer and vegan eats and hosting various events, including film screenings and gigs.

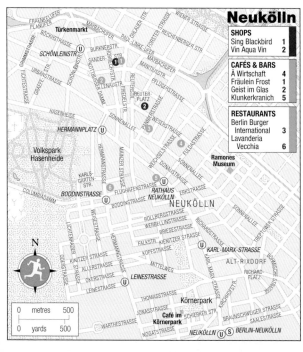

Neukölln

SHOPS	
Sing Blackbird	1
Vin Aqua Vin	2

CAFÉS & BARS	
Ä Wirtschaft	4
Fräulein Frost	1
Geist im Glas	2
Klunkerkranich	5

RESTAURANTS	
Berlin Burger International	3
Lavanderia Vecchia	6

Shops

Sing Blackbird

MAP PAGE 117, POCKET MAP K8
Sanderstr. 11 ⓤ Schönleinstr. ⓣ 030 54
84 50 51.
Housed in a former phone-sex HQ,
Sing Blackbird has the edge over
other secondhand clothes stores
thanks to a savvy selection that
favours vintage garments from the
1970s, 1980s and 1990s. They also
host occasional flea markets.

Vin Aqua Vin

MAP PAGE 117, POCKET MAP K9
Weserstr. 204 ⓤ Hermannplatz
ⓦ vinaquavin.de.
This sophisticated wine shop and
bar has introduced a new level of
sophistication to this famously
hipster street. In addition to a fine
selection of international wines
(many available by the glass), there's
a roaring fireplace for the colder
months, Chesterfield armchairs and
a dining table out back for tastings
and private dinner events.

Restaurants

Berlin Burger International

MAP PAGE 117, POCKET MAP K9
Pannierstr. 5 ⓤ Hermannplatz ⓣ 016 04
82 65 05.
There can never be enough burger
joints in Berlin, it seems. This tiny
space – just a long food bar and
a smattering of outdoor picnic
tables – lures punters in with fresh
ingredients and generous portions:
the BBI burger is enormous. €

Lavanderia Vecchia

MAP PAGE 117, POCKET MAP K9
Flughafenstr. 46 ⓤ Boddinstrasse
ⓦ lavanderiavecchia.wordpress.com.
This Italian spot reached cult
status pretty quickly after opening
in 2013, chiefly for its evening
set menus, which consist of
antipasti, *primi*, *secondi* and *dolci*.
The delicious and abundant food
is worth every penny, while the
lighter lunch deals are much
cheaper. Evening reservations

Klunkerkranich

The Körnerpark

essential. Small courtyard garden at the back. €€€€

Cafés and bars

Ä Wirtschaft

MAP PAGE 117, POCKET MAP L9
Weserstr. 40 ⓤ Rathaus Neukölln ⓦ ae-neukoelln.de.

One of the first of many informal bars to open up on boho Weserstrasse, the *Ä Bar* still holds its own as a meeting point for young creative types, expats and locals. Flea-market decor, dim lighting and table football give it a classic Berlin dive-bar atmosphere, matched to a soundtrack of indie and electro and occasional acoustic gigs from international bands.

Fräulein Frost

MAP PAGE 117, POCKET MAP K6
Friedelstr. 39 ⓤ Schönleinstr. ⓣ 030 95 59 55 21.

One of the district's best-loved ice cream shops, the Frosty Fräulein serves up delicious cones and tubs of *bioeis*, as well as sweet and savoury waffles. In summer, the outdoor patio provides a meeting point for hipsters, couples and local families. €

Geist im Glas

MAP PAGE 117, POCKET MAP K9
Lenaustr. 27 ⓤ Hermannplatz ⓦ geistimglas.de.

This trendy bar prides itself on its large selection of infused spirits that are skilfully mixed into Prohibition-era-inspired cocktails. Saturday and Sunday, there's a "Southern American" brunch with *huevos rancheros*, fluffy pancakes loaded with *dulce de leche* and lots of caramelized bacon.

Klunkerkranich

MAP PAGE 117, POCKET MAP L9
Karl-Marx-Str. 66 ⓤ Rathaus Neukölln ⓦ klunkerkranich.org.

This shabby-chic rooftop hangout is hidden on top of a distinctly unglamorous shopping centre. The urban bar vibe is complemented by a sandy floor, great views over the city and occasional concerts and film screenings. There's also two dancefloors.

Charlottenburg

Part of the four boroughs that make up City West (along with Wilmersdorf, Schöneberg and Tiergarten) Charlottenburg has long been the beating heart of West Berlin and remains so today. Known for its wealthy residents and expensive shops, it's generally dismissed by the more boho east and has much more in common with cities like London, Paris or Milan. The area's main artery, Kurfürstendamm (Ku'damm as it's colloquially known), which takes its name from the former Kurfürsten (Electors) of the Holy Roman Empire, is one of the most famous avenues in the city. It's often described as the city's Champs-Élysées, but the abundance of shops and relative dearth of impressive architecture makes it feel more like London's Oxford Street. However, many of the streets that run between Ku'damm and Kantstrasse have a charm of their own, with a wealth of independent cafés, bars, restaurants, bookstores and boutiques. The area is also home to some of the city's major sights such as Berlin's zoo and aquarium, Schloss Charlottenburg, the Kaiser Wilhelm Memorial Church and the Käthe Kollwitz Museum.

Berlin Zoo

MAP PAGE 122, POCKET MAP B6
Hardenbergplatz 8 ① / ⑤ Zoologischer
Garten ⓦ zoo-berlin.de. Charge
(combination ticket with Berlin Aquarium
available).

Berlin's zoo is Germany's oldest and one of the world's most popular, attracting (along with the adjacent aquarium) almost four million visitors in 2023. It opened in 1844 with animals donated by the royal family but was decimated during World War II, leaving only 91 surviving animals. It now houses over eighteen thousand animals spanning a thousand species. The hippo house is a highlight, while famous residents include the world's oldest gorilla: 67-year-old Fatou.

Berlin Aquarium

MAP PAGE 122, POCKET MAP C6
Budapester Str. 32 ① / ⑤ Zoologischer
Garten ⓦ aquarium-berlin.de. Charge
(combination ticket with Berlin Zoo
available).

Situated next to the zoo, the city's impressive aquarium holds the title for world's most biodiverse collection. From jellyfish to crocodiles and other reptiles and tropical fish, the aquarium has over nine thousand creatures on three floors. Built in 1913, the aquarium has retained its old-fashioned appearance, albeit incorporating modern elements.

Museum für Fotografie

MAP PAGE 122, POCKET MAP B6
Jebensstr. 2 ① / ⑤ Zoologischer Garten
ⓦ smb.museum/mf. Charge.

The Museum of Photography opened in 2004 in a former casino building, and has quickly risen in popularity, drawing about

120,000 visitors a year. The city's largest museum dedicated to the art form, it covers 2000 square metres and houses a thousand images by famous *Vogue* photographer Helmut Newton, whose provocative black-and-white photographs made him famous in the world of fashion photography and beyond; his work is shown on a rotating basis in addition to exhibits of other photographers. In the large Kaisersaal, on the second floor, you'll find the Kunstbibliothek's collection, which explores all kinds of photography ranging from the nineteenth to twenty-first centuries.

C/O Berlin (Amerika Haus)

MAP PAGE 122, POCKET MAP B6
Hardenbergstr. 22–24 ⓤ Zoologischer Garten ⓦ co-berlin.org. Charge.
Since its foundation back in 2000, C/O Berlin has hosted some of the city's best **photography exhibitions**, with shows featuring international heavyweights such as Martin Parr, Annie Leibovitz, Rene Burri and Karl Lagerfeld. In 2014, C/O Berlin moved from Mitte to West Berlin's Amerika Haus, where it hosted open-air exhibitions until the venue's reopening later that year. Visitors can expect a high standard of curation and big-name retrospectives, as well as continued promotion of young and new local talent.

Kaiser-Wilhelm-Gedächtnis-Kirche

MAP PAGE 122, POCKET MAP B7
Breitscheidplatz ⓤ Kurfürstendamm ⓦ gedaechtniskirche-berlin.de. Free.
The Kaiser Wilhelm Memorial Church, built between 1891 and 1895 in **neo-Romanesque style** by architect Franz Schwechten, was commissioned by Kaiser Wilhelm II and served as a symbol of Prussian unity. Nearly destroyed during a World War II air raid, all that remains are the ruins of the spire and entrance hall. A new structure was built in 1961,

Berlin Zoo inhabitant

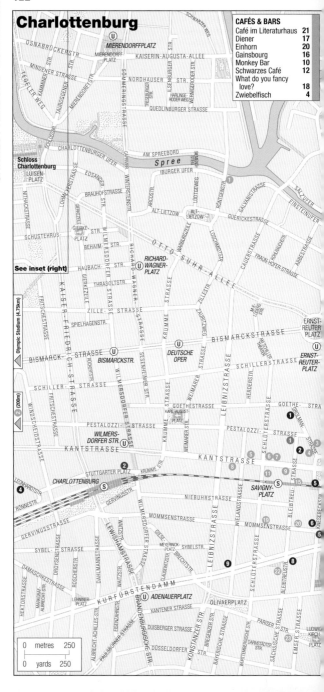

Charlottenburg

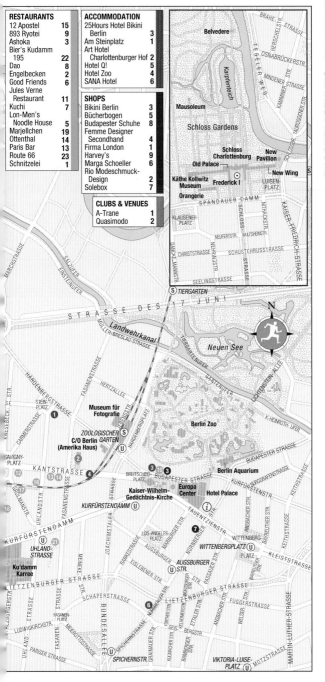

RESTAURANTS

12 Apostel	15
893 Ryotei	9
Ashoka	3
Bier's Kudamm 195	22
Dao	8
Engelbecken	2
Good Friends	6
Jules Verne Restaurant	11
Kuchi	7
Lon-Men's Noodle House	5
Marjellchen	19
Ottenthal	14
Paris Bar	13
Route 66	23
Schnitzelei	1

ACCOMMODATION

25Hours Hotel Bikini Berlin	3
Am Steinplatz	1
Art Hotel Charlottenburger Hof	2
Hotel Q!	5
Hotel Zoo	4
SANA Hotel	6

SHOPS

Bikini Berlin	3
Bücherbogen	5
Budapester Schuhe	8
Femme Designer Secondhand	4
Firma London	1
Harvey's	9
Marga Schoeller	6
Rio Modeschmuck-Design	2
Solebox	7

CLUBS & VENUES

A-Trane	1
Quasimodo	2

Schloss Charlottenburg

and the stunning, blue stained-glass windows fitted in concrete bricks contrast memorably with the haunting skeleton of the old. The base of the old spire and entrance hall is now a memorial hall, with exhibits documenting the old church through photos and artefacts that survived the bombing.

Käthe Kollwitz Museum

MAP PAGE 122, POCKET MAP A5
Spandauer Damm 10 ⓈWestend Ⓦkaetheollwitz.berlin. Charge.

German artist Käthe Kollwitz's work was greatly influenced by the loss of her son in World War I and her grandson in World War II. A pacifist who lived in Berlin for fifty years, she was the first woman elected to the Prussian Academy of the Arts but resigned her post in 1933 in protest at Hitler's rise to power. Kollwitz's works were banned by the Nazis. Many of her pieces are powerful reminders of some of the most

painful aspects of her life. Works on display here include dour self-portraits, plaintively titled sketches, woodcuts, lithographs, war protest posters and sculptures. Previously located in the oldest private home on Fasanenstrasse, the museum relocated in 2022 to its new home of the Theatre Building on the grounds of Schloss Charlottenburg.

Schloss Charlottenburg

MAP PAGE 122, POCKET MAP A5
Spandauer Damm 10–22 ⓊSophie-Charlotte-Platz/Richard-Wagner-Platz Ⓦspsg.de. Charge.

As you walk through Schloss Charlottenburg, you'll be in no doubt as to why its builder, Frederick I, was known as an extravagant spender who nearly bankrupted the state. The former Elector of Brandenburg, who named himself king of Prussia in 1701, had this ornate Baroque palace built as a summer home for his wife, Sophie Charlotte, in 1695. It started as a relatively modest dwelling but ballooned to its present palatial status with additions throughout the 1700s. Majestic rooms, art and plenty of porcelain characterize the interiors. In fact, the art in the palace constitutes the largest collection of eighteenth-century French paintings outside of France. Combined or single tickets are available for the three main buildings; the **Old Palace** features Baroque rooms, royal apartments, Chinese and Japanese porcelain and silverware chambers; the **New Wing** is more Rococo with an array of refined furniture in apartments built by Frederick the Great; and the Schinkel-built **New Pavilion** features a collection of arts and crafts. Visitors can also visit the **Mausoleum**, which contains the graves of, and memorials to, members of the Hohenzollern family, and the **Belvedere**, which displays a collection of Berlin porcelain. The reconstructed

Orangerie is also open for concerts and the gardens are open and free. Guided tours are offered of the historic apartments and chapel.

Olympic Stadium

MAP PAGE 122, POCKET MAP A5
Olympischer Platz 3 ⓢ Olympiastadion
ⓦ olympiastadion-berlin.de. Closed on days of concerts and games. Charge.
Berlin's Olympic stadium, built for the 1936 Summer Olympics (immortalized in the film *Olympia* by Leni Riefenstahl), is one of the last surviving remnants of Nazi architecture in Berlin. Occupied by the British military following the war and used by them until 1994, the stadium is now used for concerts and events and also as the official ground of Hertha BSC, Berlin's most famous football club. It was renovated for the 2006 World Cup and now has the highest all-seated capacity in Germany (74,475). The stadium remains an impressive place to visit.

Olympic Stadium

Shops

Bikini Berlin

MAP PAGE 122, POCKET MAP B6
Budapester Str. 38–50 Ⓤ/Ⓢ Zoologischer Garten Ⓦ bikiniberlin.de.
This trendy concept mall in a 1950s building place was, arguably, the place that put West Berlin back on the map. Spanning offices and a cinema, as well as the *25hours* hotel and bar (see pages 148 and 131), the lower three floors of the Bikinihaus offer chic retail and coffee stop options.

Bücherbogen

MAP PAGE 122, POCKET MAP A7
Stadtbahnbogen 593 Ⓢ Savignyplatz
Ⓦ buecherbogen.com.
You could spend hours in this famed art book store, located beneath Savignyplatz S-Bahn. You'll find plenty of English-language books in the design, photography, art and theatre sections, though few in the literature section, sadly.

Budapester Schuhe

MAP PAGE 122, POCKET MAP A7
Kurfürstendamm 199 Ⓤ Uhlandstr.

Bücherbogen

Ⓦ mybudapester.com.
A spacious and well-stocked shoe shop whose wares run the gamut from reasonably priced leather classics to designer models from Prada and Tod's.

Femme Designer Secondhand

MAP PAGE 122, POCKET MAP A7
Leonhardtstr. 22 Ⓢ Charlottenburg
Ⓦ emme-designer-secondhand.de.
Classy vintage clothing elegantly displayed in a gorgeous building near Charlottenburg station. The curated selection includes blazers, bags and dresses by timeless brands.

Firma London

MAP PAGE 122, POCKET MAP A7
Grolmanstr. 15 Ⓢ Savignyplatz
Ⓦ firmalondon.berlin.
Run by former Stella McCartney designer Sandra Tietje and gallerist Florian von Holstein, this is not for the financially faint-hearted, but it does stock some gorgeous vintage furniture and accessories.

Harvey's

MAP PAGE 122, POCKET MAP A7
Kurfürstendamm 56 Ⓤ Adenauerplatz
Ⓦ harveys.berlin.
A wonderland of men's designer clothes from designers such as Comme des Garçons and Yohji Yamamoto.

Marga Schoeller

MAP PAGE 122, POCKET MAP A7
Knesebeckstr. 33 Ⓤ Uhlandstr.
Ⓦ margaschoeller.de.
Opened in 1929 by the eponymous Frau Schoeller, this bookstore, one of the longest running in Europe, was a focal point for West Berlin's postwar literary scene. Originally located on Kurfürstendamm, the shop moved to Knesebeckstr. in 1974 and continues to sell a fantastic range of German- and English-language books on poetry, theatre and philosophy as well as fiction, history and plenty of tomes about Berlin and Germany.

Stilwerk

Rio Modeschmuck-Design

MAP PAGE 122, POCKET MAP A6
Bleibtreustr. 52 Ⓢ Savignyplatz Ⓦ rio-
modeschmuck-berlin.de.
Designer Barbara Kranz opened
her jewellery store back in 1984
– she calls her creations "after
5pm" jewellery due to their natural
evening-wear flamboyance.

Solebox

MAP PAGE 122, POCKET MAP C7
Nürnbergerstr. 14 Ⓤ Wittenbergplatz
Ⓦ solebox.com.
A spacious shrine to streetwear,
stocking Reebok, Converse, Ellesse
and Adidas sneakers plus T-shirts
and hoodies.

Restaurants

12 Apostel

MAP PAGE 122, POCKET MAP A6
Bleibtreustr. 49 Ⓢ Savignyplatz Ⓦ 12-
aposteli.de/charlottenburg.
A smart, Baroque-style interior
(check the kitsch religious frescoes)
and generously sized thin pizzas
mark this place out. They're slightly
on the expensive side, but specials
on the Mon–Fri lunch menu are
good value. €€€

893 Ryotei

MAP PAGE 122, POCKET MAP A6
Kantstr. 135 Ⓢ Savignyplatz Ⓦ 893ryotei.
de.
You arrive at a seemingly rundown
building with graffitied walls, but
once inside, a Japanese low-lit
restaurant awaits you, with a large
menu offering dishes that are
inspired by Japanese, Mexican and
Peruvian cuisine, such as *Tiradito
Hiramasa* (yellowtail with Peruvian
salsa €18), a ceviche 893-style or
just simple sushi. €€€€

Ashoka

MAP PAGE 122, POCKET MAP A6
Grolmanstr. 51 Ⓢ Savignyplatz
Ⓦ myashoka.de. Daily noon–midnight.
Ashok Sharma opened this
restaurant in 1975 as he was
missing the food from his home in
Punjab. It offers well-priced, decent
quality food in a small *Imbiss*-style
place. Vegetarian options and
friendly staff. €

Wiener schnitzel

Bier's Kudamm 195

MAP PAGE 122, POCKET MAP A7
Kurfürstendamm 195 Ⓤ Uhlandstr.
Ⓦ biers-currywurst.de.

One of several spots claimed as the "best in Berlin" for *Currywurst*. It also serves meat skewers and meatballs and is generally busy all night; if you feel like splashing out ask for champagne with your *Wurst*. €

Dao

MAP PAGE 122, POCKET MAP A6
Kantstr. 133 Ⓢ Savignyplatz Ⓦ dao-
restaurant.de. Daily noon–11pm.

Opened by a Berliner and his Thai wife, Dao, in the 1970s, this Thai spot serves dishes brimful of flavour. Alongside *pad Thai* and fish and duck dishes there are specials like "Bloodnoodlesoup". €

Engelbecken

MAP PAGE 122, POCKET MAP A6
Witzlebenstr. 31 Ⓤ Sophie-Charlotte-Platz
Ⓦ engelbecken.de.

A high-quality restaurant that serves Bavarian and Alpine cuisine – *schnitzel*, goulash – with an emphasis on organic products and homemade sauces. Vegetarian and vegan options are available, and the park-facing terrace is nice in the summer. €€€

Good Friends

MAP PAGE 122, POCKET MAP A6
Kantstr. 30 Ⓢ Savignyplatz Ⓦ goodfriends-
berlin.de.

One of Berlin's few really authentic Cantonese restaurants, with plain decor and a full range of classics. It's always busy; evening bookings recommended. €€€

Jules Verne Restaurant

MAP PAGE 122, POCKET MAP A6
Schlüterstr. 61 Ⓢ Savignyplatz Ⓦ jules-
verne-berlin.de.

The interior feels classic French but the menu is aptly global, ranging from *Flammen* (*tarte flambée*) and *schnitzel* to *couscous* and *satay*. Lunchtime deals change daily. €€

Kuchi

MAP PAGE 122, POCKET MAP A6
Kantstr. 30 Ⓢ Savignyplatz Ⓦ kuchi.de.
Daily noon–midnight.

With sister restaurants in Mitte and Kreuzberg, this place sells the same range of innovative sushi, *sashimi* and *yakitori*, as well as some Thai, Chinese and Korean dishes. Busy at peak times, so it's best to reserve a table. €€

Lon-Men's Noodle House

MAP PAGE 122, POCKET MAP A6
Kantstr. 33 Ⓢ Savignyplatz ☎ 030 31 51 96 78.

Tiny Taiwanese noodle shop run by a friendly family who make excellent dumplings and noodle soups (small and large portions available). €

Marjellchen

MAP PAGE 122, POCKET MAP A7
Mommsenstr. 9 Ⓢ Savignyplatz
Ⓦ restaurant-marjellchen-berlin.de.

It's obvious from the window displays – books, photos and other paraphernalia – that this is a time warp kind of place. Indeed, *Marjellchen* specializes in cuisine from East Prussia, Pomerania and Silesia, all served up in a cosy, traditional atmosphere. Portions are generous and service is friendly. €€€

Ottenthal

MAP PAGE 122, POCKET MAP B6
Kantstr. 153 Ⓢ Savignyplatz Ⓦ ottenthal. com.

White-clothed tables and relatively sparse white walls lend this place an unfussy, classic feel that ties in well with the Austrian cuisine – which is simple yet some of the best in the area. Organic ingredients feature on the menu, which includes fish dishes, roast deer and a famed *Wiener schnitzel*. Good Austrian wine list too. €€€€

Paris Bar

MAP PAGE 122, POCKET MAP B6
Kantstr. 152 Ⓢ/Ⓤ Zoologischer Garten
Ⓦ parisbar.net.

There's still something tangibly bohemian about the *Paris Bar*, once one of the centres of West Berlin's art scene until the Wall fell and the East took over. Interesting artworks vie for your attention and the somewhat pricey food takes second place to the social networking action. €€€€

Route 66

MAP PAGE 122, POCKET MAP A7
Pariser Str 44. Ⓤ Hohenzollernplatz.
Ⓦ route66diner.de.

A traditional '50s American diner filled with jukeboxes, red booths and bar stools and pictures of all the icons, like Elvis, the cast of Grease and other flashy neon signs. If you are in need of a real burger with a thick milkshake or some ribs, this is the place to be. €€€

Schnitzelei

MAP PAGE 122, POCKET MAP A5
Röntgen Str. 7 Ⓤ Richard-Wagner-Platz
Ⓦ schnitzelei.de.

Café im Literaturhaus

Quasimodo

The name gives it away: if you are a lover of the Austro-German cuisine, this is schnitzel heaven, located on the edge of the river Spree with a nice beer garden for Berlin summer evenings. A simple restaurant, which – in addition to schnitzels – serves a variety of 'German tapas' dishes like *Königsberger Klopse* (meatballs with caper sauce) or plums wrapped in bacon. €€€

Cafés and bars

Café im Literaturhaus
MAP PAGE 122, POCKET MAP B7
Fasanenstr. 23 ⓤ Uhlandstr.
ⓦ literaturhaus-berlin.de.
This place is every bit as classic and elegant as its name suggests. The spacious interior or beautiful summer garden are great spots for coffee and cake, lunch or dinner: the largely organic menu changes

regularly and has vegetarian options. €

Diener
MAP PAGE 122, POCKET MAP A6
Grolmanstr. 47 ⓢ Savignyplatz ⓦ diener-berlin.de.
This Berlin ale house is a local institution – not only because it was opened in 1954 by former German heavyweight boxer Franz Diener, but because it serves dishes like *Königsberger Klopse* (meatballs in white sauce with capers) and has an atmosphere as old school as the menu. €

Einhorn
MAP PAGE 122, POCKET MAP A7
Mommsenstr. 2 ⓢ Savignyplatz
ⓦ einhorn-deli.de.
A great place if you're seeking a tasty veggie lunch. There's a buffet selection including antipasti and dishes like lentils with goat's cheese. €

Gainsbourg

MAP PAGE 122, POCKET MAP A6
Jeanne-Mammen-Bogen 576–577
Ⓢ Savignyplatz Ⓦ gainsbourg-bar-berlin.
com.

The name may pay homage to
the master of risqué *chanson*, but
the cocktails and food are more
mainstream. Nevertheless, the
drinks are some of the best in the
neighbourhood.

Monkey Bar

MAP PAGE 122, POCKET MAP B6
Budapesterstr. 40 Ⓤ/Ⓢ Zoologischer
Garten Ⓦ monkeybarberlin.de.

This rooftop bar in West Berlin
is found at the *25hours* hotel (see
page 148), making it an even
more exciting place to stay. The
floor-to-ceiling windows make for
great sundowner vibes.

Schwarzes Café

MAP PAGE 122, POCKET MAP A6
Kantstr. 148 Ⓢ Savignyplatz
Ⓦ schwarzescafe-berlin.de.

The slightly ragged charm of the
"Black Café" makes it feel like
it would be better placed in the
east. The downstairs is small and
intimate, but upstairs the large, airy
room has a relaxed, convivial vibe.
Food is served 24 hours, including
breakfasts – but this is a night-owl
place really. €

What do you fancy love?

MAP PAGE 122, POCKET MAP A7
Knesebeckstr. 68–69 Ⓤ Uhlandstrasse
Ⓦ whatdoyoufancylove.de.

Modern café for house-
made muesli, top bagels and
freshly juiced juices. Cosy yet
cool, they're known for their
showstopping cakes, which can
be made to order (and customer
designs). €

Zwiebelfisch

MAP PAGE 122, POCKET MAP A6
Savignyplatz 7 Ⓢ Savignyplatz
Ⓦ zwiebelfisch-berlin.de.

Corner bar and 1970s throwback
for would-be arty and intellectual
types. Jazz, earnest debate and good
cheap grub, including goulash and
Swabian Maultaschen, served until
1am. €

Clubs and venues

A-Trane

MAP PAGE 122, POCKET MAP A6
Bleibtreustr. 1 Ⓢ Savignyplatz Ⓦ a-trane.
de.

Good jazz and decent cocktails in
a classic jazz-style interior (small
and smoky). Often hosts major
international acts. Music from
about 8pm.

Quasimodo

MAP PAGE 122, POCKET MAP B6
Kantstr. 12A Ⓤ Savignyplatz
Ⓦ quasimodo.de.

A classic jazz bar, *Quasimodo*
(underneath the Delphi Cinema)
features black-and-white photos,
low ceilings and intimate tables.
Aside from jazz, there's funk,
blues and Latin and the odd
international star.

Schwarzes Café

Schöneberg

Famous during the 1920s as the centre of Berlin's decadent nightlife scene and again in the 1970s when it was home to David Bowie during his dissipated sojourn in the city, Schöneberg's star waned in the 1990s as the cool kids moved east. But while East Berlin has become increasingly slick and unaffordable, this part of town has – as they say – kept it real. Nowadays the hipsters are heading back, attracted by the still-low rents and the burgeoning gallery scene in Potsdamer Strasse, and it maintains its reputation as the queerest borough in Berlin, especially around Nollendorfplatz. It's also long been a popular spot for writers – Christopher Isherwood had his digs in Nollendorfstrasse back in the day, and a new generation of writers including Helen DeWitt and Ida Hattemer-Higgins have called the neighbourhood home. Though it lacks any major sights, the charming Winterfeldtplatz hosts a highly popular farmers' market (Sat 8am–4pm).

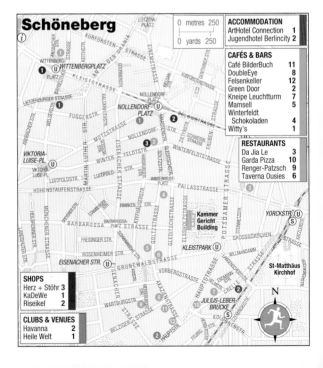

Schöneberg

ACCOMMODATION	
ArtHotel Connection	1
Jugendhotel Berlincity	2

CAFÉS & BARS	
Café BilderBuch	11
DoubleEye	8
Felsenkeller	12
Green Door	2
Kneipe Leuchtturm	7
Mamsell	5
Winterfeldt Schokoladen	4
Witty's	1

RESTAURANTS	
Da Jia Le	3
Garda Pizza	10
Renger-Patzsch	9
Taverna Ousies	6

SHOPS	
Herz + Stöhr	3
KaDeWe	1
Riseikel	2

CLUBS & VENUES	
Havanna	2
Heile Welt	1

Nollendorfplatz U-Bahn station

Shops

Herz + Stöhr

MAP PAGE 132, POCKET MAP D8
Winterfeldtstr. 52 ⓤ Nollendorfplatz
ⓦ herzundstoehr.com.
Intelligent, elegant designs from
this German fashion duo – the
dresses and suits are grown-up but
not dowdy, and everything can be
altered to fit.

KaDeWe

MAP PAGE 132, POCKET MAP C7
Tauentzienstr. 21–24 ⓤ Wittenbergplatz
ⓦ kadewe.de.
If you're tired of Berlin's austere side,
check out KaDeWe (Kaufhaus Des
Westerns), a temple to conspicuous
consumption. The second-largest
department store in continental
Europe, it sports designer gear
alongside some surprisingly
affordable accessories and
homewares. The legendary sixth-
floor food hall will leave all but the
most jaded of foodies starry-eyed.

Riseikel

MAP PAGE 132, POCKET MAP D7
Bülowstr. 5 ⓤ Nollendorfplatz ⓦ riseikel.de.
Formerly known as Mr Dead &
Ms Free, a dusty little legend of

a music shop crammed full of
everything from the latest imports
to rare albums.

Restaurants

Da Jia Le

MAP PAGE 132, POCKET MAP D9
Goebenstr. 23 ⓤ / ⓢ Yorckstrasse
ⓦ dajiale-berlin.de
Acclaimed Chinese restaurant
specialising in Dongbei cuisine from
the country's northeast. Laid-back
dining room with serious cooking
and food served family style. Dishes
like the hotpot – starring spareribs,
beans and corn tortillas – offer an
authentic taste of China you may
not have tried before. €€

Garda Pizza

MAP PAGE 132, POCKET MAP D9
Crellestr. 48 ⓢ Julius-Leber-Brücke ⓣ 030
78 09 79 70.
Locals flock to *Garda Pizza* for
their trays of thin-crust Roman-
style *focaccia*. Their most popular
slice combines fresh aubergine,
mushroom, sheep's salami and
artichokes. A tray will feed a
hungry group of four. Join the
crowd on the pavement or mosey
down a few metres and let your

Green Door

children burn off the calories in the neighbouring playground. €

Renger-Patzsch

MAP PAGE 132, POCKET MAP D9
Wartburgstr. 54 ⓤ Eisenacher Str.
ⓦ renger-patzsch.com.
An interior of dark wood and white tablecloths forms the backdrop to an expertly prepared selection of German dishes. In spring, look for the dandelion salad with lardons; in winter, the braised ox cheeks with bacon-wrapped plums, turnips and mashed potatoes. €€€

Taverna Ousies

MAP PAGE 132, POCKET MAP D9
Grunewaldstr. 16 ⓤ Eisenacher Str.
ⓦ taverna-ousies.de.
This kitschy, raucous Greek taverna is a perennial favourite. There are no real duds, so go wild with the meze menu and be entertained by the jolly staff. Reservations essential at weekends. €€

Cafés and bars

Café BilderBuch

MAP PAGE 132, POCKET MAP D9
Akazienstr. 28 ⓢ Julius-Leber-Brücke
ⓦ cafe-bilderbuch.de.
Lovely rambling café in the Viennese tradition. It doesn't look particularly special from outside, but the comfortable back parlour may well hold you captive for hours. Great breakfasts lovely cakes, elegant coffees and courtyard seating, too. €

DoubleEye

MAP PAGE 132, POCKET MAP D8
Akazienstr. 22 ⓤ Eisenacher Str.
ⓦ doubleeye.de.
This cosy café offers some of the most delicious coffee in the neighbourhood – not to mention friendly service and great pastries. Good people-watching, too. €

Felsenkeller

MAP PAGE 132, POCKET MAP D9
Akazienstr. 2 ⓢ Julius-Leber-Brücke
ⓣ 030 78 13 447.
The perfect destination when you're nostalgic for old Berlin. Founded in 1923, this bar is famous for its eight beers on tap, drawn the old-fashioned way. There's hearty, simple food, such as lentil soup and swede stew. No music, but plenty of atmosphere. €

Green Door

MAP PAGE 132, POCKET MAP D8
Winterfeldtstr. 50 ⓤ Nollendorfplatz
ⓦ greendoor.de.

Ring the bell and enter one of Berlin's best-loved cocktail bars. The expert but unpretentious staff will recommend the perfect drink. An older crowd fills the cosy room.

Kneipe Leuchtturm

MAP PAGE 132, POCKET MAP D9
Crellestr. 41 ⓤ Kleistpark ⓦ leuchtturm-kneipe.de.

If you think beer just isn't the same without a cigarette, head for the "Lighthouse", with its unpretentious, welcoming atmosphere favoured by former hippies and locals. The wines can be middling so go for one of the beers on tap.

Mamsell

MAP PAGE 132, POCKET MAP D8
Goltzstr. 48 ⓤ Eisenacher Str.
ⓦ mamsellberlin.de.

Those with a penchant for pink will be delighted by this sweet café/shop. The addictive real hot chocolate is served with a dusting of freshly grated ginger. €

Winterfeldt Schokoladen

MAP PAGE 132, POCKET MAP D8
Goltzstr. 23 ⓤ Nollendorfplatz
ⓦ winterfeldt-schokoladen.de.

Once an apothecary, this café-chocolate shop serves a lovely selection of pastries to cure all your ills. Scones with clotted cream and jam and warm chocolate fondant cake are popular. €

Witty's

MAP PAGE 132, POCKET MAP C7
Wittenbergplatz 5 ⓤ Wittenbergplatz
ⓦ wittys.de.

One of the city's first and finest organic sausage stands, *Witty's* has customers lined up along the square for their *Currywurst* and crispy fries. €

Clubs and venues

Havanna

MAP PAGE 132, POCKET MAP D9
Hauptstr. 30 Ⓢ Julius-Leber-Brücke
ⓦ havanna-berlin.de.

With four floors and seven bars, this magnet for Latin American music fans draws a diverse clientele. Serious salsa and tango fans will find like-minded devotees to shake it with on the dancefloor.

Heile Welt

MAP PAGE 132, POCKET MAP D7
Motzstr. 5 ⓤ Nollendorfplatz ⓣ 030 21 91 75 07.

A much-beloved destination for gay men. Music runs the gamut from soul and dance to house and home-brewed "Schlager". During the week, enjoy one of the friendly bar staff's famously strong cocktails and settle into a comfortable sofa. The action picks up at the weekend, when it gets too crowded for some, and just right for others.

KaDeWe

Day-trips from Berlin

There's so much to do in Berlin that it's easy to forget there's a world outside the city. Berlin's surroundings are surprisingly sparse and beautiful – a bucolic swathe of lakes, forests and small villages. Amidst the vast landscape lie some of the city's highlights, many of them less than an hour from the centre. Easily accessible by public transport, areas such as Dahlem, Potsdam and Wannsee make for enjoyable and edifying visits (as well as offering memorials to the darker side of the city's past). The most popular day-trip is Potsdam, which includes Schloss Sanssouci and Babelsberg film studios as well as a town centre distinct from anything in Berlin. The Wannsee area offers lakeside beaches as well as historical villas and the magical Pfaueninsel, while Dahlem has botanical gardens and the Museum of European Cultures. All visitors will find journeys to Sachsenhausen concentration camp, Villa Wannsee and Hohenschönhausen Stasi prison both chilling and instructive.

Sachsenhausen

Str. der Nationen 22, Oranienburg
Ⓢ Oranienburg Ⓦ stiftung-bg.de. Free; charge for guided tours.

Located in Oranienburg, 35km north of the city, Sachsenhausen ranks among Berlin's most emotionally wrenching wartime memorials – which is saying a lot for a city like this. Established in 1936, it was first used as a prison for political opponents. It became a training ground for SS officers, and from 1938 to 1945 the central administration for all concentration camps was located here. After the war started, prisoners from all over Europe were brought here. In 1943 a small gas chamber was added. By 1945 some 200,000 people had passed through the prison, with tens of thousands dying of starvation, disease, mistreatment or murdered systematically by the SS. In April 1945 more than 33,000 prisoners were sent on the notorious death marches, during which more than a thousand died – those who collapsed en route were routinely shot. When the camp was liberated by Russian soldiers on April 22, 1945, only three thousand prisoners remained, many of whom died in the days afterwards. The camp became a Soviet-run prison named "Special Camp No. 7" (renamed in 1948 to "Special Camp No. 1"). Sixty thousand people were interned here over five years, including six thousand German officers transferred from Western Allied POW camps. By the time the camp closed in the spring of 1950, twelve thousand had died of malnutrition and disease. In 1961, the GDR turned the site into a memorial, removing many of the original buildings and constructing an obelisk, statue and meeting area. Today the memorial is a place of commemoration as well as a **museum** that includes a wealth of information on the camp, artwork by inmates, models, pictures and more. Following the discovery in 1990 of mass graves from the Soviet period, a separate museum was opened about the Soviet-era history.

Potsdam

Direct line to Wannsee, then change on S7 (20–30min; ticket for zones A,B and C); or regional trains (RE1) to Potsdam and Babelsburg. You can cover most of Potsdam on foot, though the Berlin and Potsdam WelcomeCard (see page 154), available from the tourist centre at the train station, includes transport and gives discounts on over two hundred attractions. Ⓦ potsdam-tourism.com.

Located 24km southwest of Berlin, Potsdam makes for an easy and pleasant day-trip, with plenty to see and do, from the wonderful Schloss Sanssouci and its gardens to the Babelsberg film studios. There are two quaint historic quarters in the city itself that are worth seeking out. The **Russian Colony Alexandrowka** (Alexandrowka 2; Ⓦ alexandrowka. de; charge), created in 1826–27 at the request of Friedrich Wilhelm III in memory of his friend Tsar Alexander I, is an artist's village with twelve picturesque wooden houses and a small Russian Orthodox chapel (1829) on Kapellenberg hill to the north. Check out the Russian tearoom in the warden's house. The **Holländisches Viertel**, or Dutch quarter, consists of around 150 three-storey redbrick houses and was built between 1734 and 1742 for Dutch craftsmen invited to Potsdam by Friedrich Wilhelm I. The houses are built in the classic Dutch style with shuttered windows and slanted roofs; at Mittelstrasse 8 the **Jan Bouman Haus** preserves a typical house of the era (Ⓦ jan-bouman-haus. de; charge), while the **Potsdam Museum** at Alter Markt 9 (Ⓦ potsdam-museum.de; charge) displays historic paintings and photos of the city.

Museum Barberini

Humboldtstr. 5–6 Ⓦ museum-barberini. de. Charge.

In January 2017, the **Museum Barberini** opened inside Frederick the Great's former Barberini

The Havel River in Potsdam

Schloss Sanssouci

Palace on the Alter Markt. As well as exhibiting a permanent collection of works from the former GDR, the museum also hosts three temporary exhibitions per year, ranging in aesthetic scope from Old Masters to contemporary art.

Schloss Sanssouci and park

Park Sanssouci ⑤ Potsdam. Around 5km from Potsdam train station; bus #695 goes from the train station, with stops at Schloss Sanssouci, the Orangerie and Neues Palais (among others). ⓦ spsg.de. Palace: timed guided tours only; charge. Park: free.

The highlight of any trip to Potsdam, Schloss Sanssouci was built for Frederick the Great by the magnificently titled Georg Wenzeslaus von Knobelsdorff between 1745 and 1747. It was his summer residence – the place he came for some peace and quiet and to be with his beloved dogs (*Sans Souci* means "without worries" in French); parts of the park, buildings and palaces dotted around it were added to

by later Prussian kings. Having survived unscathed from the War, the palace is considered one of the most significant examples of Rococo architecture – much of the original artworks were moved to Rheinsberg during the War or were transferred as booty to the Soviet Union, though Frederick's library and 36 oil paintings were returned and can be viewed today alongside furnishings and decorations from the original rooms. The adjacent **picture gallery** exhibits works by Rubens, van Dyck, Caravaggio and other renowned artists, and the historic windmill – built in the Dutch style and rebuilt in 1993 – is worth a visit, as is the **Chinese House** (same times as Sanssouci; charge) and the **New Palace** (Neues Palais; charge), a larger Baroque-style palace intended to display Frederick's power to the world. Best of all is the surrounding **park**, an inspiring display of terraced vineyards, flamboyant flower beds, hedges and abundant fruit trees. Note that the palaces are highly popular in summer and tours inside the main palace are limited, so arrive early or book ahead.

Filmpark Babelsberg

Grossbeerenstr. 200 ⓢ Babelsburg, then bus #601, #619, #690 to Filmpark or RE1 to Medienstadt ⓦ filmpark-babelsberg. de. Charge.

Some of Germany's most famous films were created at Studio Babelsberg, including masterpieces such as *Metropolis* (1927) and *The Blue Angel* (1930), starring Marlene Dietrich – in its heyday the studios were Europe's version of Hollywood. This associated theme park allows visitors to roam sets from old films, witness stuntmen in action and marvel at the special effects. It's especially good (if not better) for kids, who will enjoy the adventure playground.

Museum Europäischer Kulturen (MEK)

Arnimallee 25, a short signposted walk down Iltisstrasse directly opposite ⓤ Dahlem-Dorf ⓦ smb.museum/mek. Charge.

The **Museum Europäischer Kulturen** (Museum of European Cultures) is devoted to the everyday lives and culture of people in Europe. With around 280,000 cultural-historical objects, its collection provides a unique insight into European everyday culture and popular art. The permanent exhibition "Cultural Contacts: Living in Europe" provides a cross-section of the rich collection of the MEK and deals with discussions on social movements and national boundaries in Europe.

Domäne Dahlem

Königin-Luise-Str. 49 (just west of and over the road from ⓤ Dahlemdorf) ⓦ domaene-dahlem.de. Charge.

A working farm and handicrafts centre, **Domäne Dahlem** attempts to show off the lifestyle and skills of the pre-industrial age.

The old estate house has a few odds and ends, most intriguing of which are the thirteenth-century swastikas, but the collection of agricultural instruments in an outbuilding is more comprehensive. Elsewhere there are ponies, turkeys, pigs, sheep and cows in the grounds, and demonstrations of woodcarving, wool- and cotton-spinning and various other farm crafts. At weekends some of the old agricultural machinery is fired up and the animals are paraded. The complex also now features the **Culinarium**: a kid-friendly, interactive cultural history of food – from farm to fork – complete with locally produced goods to buy. A visit out here is best combined with a visit to the nearby **Museum Europäischer Kulturen** and/or the city's **Botanical Garden**.

Dahlem Botanic Garden and Botanical Museum

Königin-Luise-Str. 6–8 ⓤ/ⓢ Rathaus Steglitz, and 15min walk or bus #X83 to Königin-Luise-Str./Botanischer Garten ⓦ bgbm.org. Charge.

Founded as an extension to the kitchen garden of the Berlin palace by the Elector of Brandenburg, by 1815 the royal herbarium had developed hugely thanks to extensive botanical research by C.L. Willdenow. The collection was moved to Dahlem 1897–1910 and today hosts 20,000 species of plants over 43 hectares, making it one of the largest and most diverse botanical gardens in the world. The sixteen greenhouses (Gewächshäuser) feature an array of specialist areas such as desert and rainforest. The garden resembles a planted map with "Prairie", "Himalaya" and "Alps" sections topped by aquatic and marsh plants, an aroma and touch garden and medicinal plants. The attached museum features sections of preserved fossils and plant formations on artificially constructed landscapes.

Pfaueninsel

Ⓢ Wannsee, then bus #218 to the passenger ferry (charge, inc. entry to the island). Ⓦ spsg.de Castle: charge. Island: charge inc. ferry.

Formerly known as *Kanninchenwerder* ("Rabbit Island"), Peacock Island features a castle built by Prussian king Frederick William II in 1793 for him and his mistress Wilhelmine Enke. His successor Frederick William III turned the island into a model farm and from 1816 had the park redesigned by Peter Joseph Lenné. Karl Friedrich Schinkel also planned a few of the buildings, for example the former Palm House and Llama House, and also the Cavalier House in the middle of the island. The king also laid out a menagerie modelled on the Ménagerie du Jardin des Plantes in Paris, in which exotic animals and birds including peacocks were housed. In addition to several free-ranging peacocks, chickens and pheasants can be found in captivity, complemented by a rich variety of

Movie props at Filmpark Babelsberg

flora. The entire island is designated as a **nature reserve**.

House of the Wannsee Conference

Ⓢ Wannsee, then bus #114 (direction "Krankenhaus Heckeshorn") to Haus der Wannsee-Konferenz Ⓦ ghwk.de. Free; charge for guided tours.

It's hard to imagine that this handsome villa at Wannsee lake has an iniquitous history, but it was here that the "Final Solution of the Jewish Question" was discussed by fifteen high-ranking Nazi officials, who agreed to exterminate the entire Jewish population of Europe. Since 1992 it has served as a memorial and documentation centre, with a permanent exhibit that draws on detailed historical research to profile the conference and the process of deporting Jews to the ghettoes and camps. A library on the second floor (named after Joseph Wulf, an Auschwitz survivor and campaigner for this memorial) holds thousands of books on Nazism, anti-Semitism and the Holocaust, as well as Nazi-era documents such as children's books promoting Nazism.

Strandbad Wannsee

Wannseebadeweg 25 Ⓢ Wannsee/ Nikolaisee Ⓦ berlinerbaeder.de. Charge.

Strandbad Wannsee's impressive 1275m long (and 80m wide) sweep of sandy beach has long been a venerable summer destination for Berliners. Officially the **largest lido in Europe**, it's located on the eastern side of the Wannsee, just a twenty-minute train ride from the city centre. Its current "look" was formulated by architects Martin Wagner and Richard Ermisch. Today the "Mother of all Lidos" attracts up to 230,000 visitors per year and has been designated a cultural heritage site. Between 2004 and 2007, it underwent a €12.5 million refurbishment for its centenary celebrations.

Strandbad Wannsee

Max Liebermann Villa

Colomierstr. 3 Ⓢ Wannsee then either bus #114 toward Heckeshorn to Liebermann-Villa (5min) or 20min walk Ⓦ liebermann-villa.de. Charge.

German Impressionist Max Liebermann's "castle by the sea", built in 1909, and particularly its expansive, 7000-square-metre garden, was the subject of more than two hundred of his paintings. An exhibition documents Liebermann's life here, with prints and photographs. On the upper floor are around forty paintings, pastels and prints that revolve around his Wannsee works – pictures of the flower terrace, perennial garden, birch grove and the lawn leading down to the lake – plus portraits of family and personalities. The garden has been reconstructed today as it was originally planned by Liebermann, and brims with rare and diverse species.

Gedenkstätte Berlin-Hohenschönhausen

Genslerstr. 66 #M5 to Freienwalder Str. (then 10min walk) or #M6 from Hackescher Markt to Genslerstr. (then 10min walk) Ⓦ stiftung-hsh.de. Entry by guided tour only. English tours 10.40am, 12.40am & 2.40pm; charge.

With its intact buildings, equipment and furniture, the Stasi prison at Hohenschönhausen provides a particularly clear – and grisly – portrait of public persecution during GDR times. The Stasi used it to detain and physically and psychologically torture dissenters. The prison, which remained largely a secret until the Wall fell in 1989, was turned into a memorial in 1994, and since 2000 has been an independent foundation that researches the history of the prison and produces exhibitions, events and publications. The only way to see the memorial is via a **guided tour**, available in German, English and other languages; tours with former inmates are also available, though mostly in German. The tour includes a survey of the older and newer prison blocks and detailed descriptions of daily life in the prison.

ACCOMMODATION

Hotel Adlon

Accommodation

Berlin's accommodation options run the gamut from cheap and cheerful hostels to corporate hotels, super-deluxe five stars and intimate boutique and "art" hotels. Prices quoted usually include taxes and service charges, though breakfast and parking are sometimes extra – it's worth double-checking when booking. While there are many rooms in the city, there are also a lot of visitors; booking ahead in the warmer, more popular months is recommended, especially during large events such as the film festival (see page 158).

Spandauer Vorstadt

CIRCUS HOSTEL MAP PAGE 28, POCKET MAP D11. Weinbergsweg 1a ⓤ Rosenthaler Platz ⓦ circus-berlin.de. One of the most popular hostels in the city, *Circus* offers pleasant, clean dorms, private rooms – even penthouse apartments – and a convivial, upbeat vibe right on buzzing Rosenthaler Platz. Bicycles for rent, walking tours and their own microbrewery add to the appeal. **€**

CIRCUS HOTEL MAP PAGE 28, POCKET MAP E10. Rosenthalerstr. 1 ⓤ Rosenthaler Platz ⓦ circus-berlin.de. The sister establishment of the *Circus* hostel (located just over the road) is a more upmarket and more eco-friendly place. Sixty rooms include junior suites and apartments, decorated in striking colours with wooden floors and a mix of antique and modern furniture. **€**

HEART OF GOLD MAP PAGE 28, POCKET MAP C12. Johannisstr. 11 ⓢ Oranienburg ⓦ heartofgold-hostel.de. Good-value and friendly hostel near one of the busiest strips in Mitte. Dorms and rooms are basic but clean, and staff go the extra mile to make staying here fun. Expect lots of space-themed decorative touches. **€**

KASTANIENHOF MAP PAGE 28, POCKET MAP H2. Kastanienallee 65 ⓤ Senefelderplatz ⓦ kastanienhof. berlin. This recently renovated hotel has 44 rooms in an elegant house, with decor that nods to Berlin's fascinating history, including photos, illustrations and maps. Great location for Prenzlauer Berg and Mitte. **€**

SOHO HOUSE MAP PAGE 28, POCKET MAP F11. Torstr. 1 ⓤ Rosa-Luxemburg-Platz ⓦ sohohouseberlin.com. Private members' club in a restored Bauhaus building with forty swanky apartments, four huge lofts and forty hotel rooms that range from tiny to extra large. Decor is quirky and fun, and hints at the faded glamour of the late 1920s. There's also a lovely spa, gym,

---

Accommodation price codes

The price codes given in this Guide are based on the **cheapest available double room for one night**, in peak season. Unless otherwise stated, **breakfast is not included**.

€ = under €120
€€ = €121–200
€€€ = €201–250
€€€€ = over €250

Apartment rentals

Private apartments are a popular and often good-value choice for many travellers to Berlin. The best apartments offer value for money, are well-located and usually stylish or interestingly decorated. Airbnb was banned from renting out complete apartments in the city in 2016 (rooms within a house are still possible), but that move has since been reversed. Also check out ⓦ brilliant-apartments.de and ⓦ ferienwohnungen.de, which offer a good spread of apartments, rooms and regular special deals.

rooftop pool, restaurant, bars, screening room and private dining area. €€€€

WEINMEISTER MAP PAGE 28, POCKET MAP E11. Weinmeisterstr. 2 ⓤ Weinmeisterstr. ⓦ the-weinmeister. com. This adults-only swish hotel features 84 spacious rooms with large beds and a stylish design ethic. There's also a decent bar and lounge, a rooftop bar and a sixth-floor beauty spa. €€

Unter den Linden and the government quarter

ADLON KEMPINSKI MAP PAGE 48, POCKET MAP B14. Unter den Linden 77 ⓤ/Ⓢ Brandenburger Tor ⓦ hotel-adlon. de. Probably the most famous hotel in the city, and definitely one of the most luxurious, the *Hotel Adlon Kempinski* matches a wealth of history (previous guests include Emperor Wilhelm II, Albert Einstein and Michael Jackson, who famously dangled his baby from one of the hotel balconies) with serious five-star swagger and an enviable location overlooking the Brandenburg Gate on Pariser Platz. €€€€

ARCOTEL JOHN F MAP PAGE 48, POCKET MAP D14. Werderscher Markt 11 ⓤ Hausvogteiplatz ⓦ arcotelhotels. com. Close to Gendarmenmarkt, this 190-room hotel is a cheaper option than the neighbouring big guns but has all the facilities you'll need – gym, sauna, meeting rooms, restaurant, bar. €€

ARTE LUISE KUNSTHOTEL MAP PAGE 48, POCKET MAP B12. Luisenstr. 19 ⓤ/

Ⓢ Friedrichstr. ⓦ luise-berlin.com. Within walking distance of the Reichstag and Unter den Linden, this art hotel has fifty charmingly appointed and highly individual rooms, Dutch sculptures in the large lobby and an in-house restaurant serving German-Mediterranean cuisine. €

HOTEL DE ROME MAP PAGE 48, POCKET MAP C14. Behrenstr. 37 ⓤ Französische Str. ⓦ roccofortehotels.com. Occupying a nineteenth-century former Dresdner Bank building, this high-class hotel mixes history with a swanky interior, luxurious rooms, an expansive spa and a fantastic restaurant (*CHIARO*) and rooftop terrace. €€€€

WESTIN GRAND MAP PAGE 48, POCKET MAP C13. Friedrichstr. 158–164 ⓤ Französische Str. ⓦ westingrandberlin. com. Built during the GDR, this large hotel, well positioned on Friedrichstrasse and close to the Brandenburg Gate, has been refurbished to feature a refined *belle époque* interior and beautifully appointed rooms and suites. €€

Alexanderplatz and the Nikolaiviertel

ART'OTEL MAP PAGE 58, POCKET MAP F14. Wallstr. 70–73 ⓤ Märkisches Museum ⓦ artotelberlinmitte.com. With its impressive range of paintings by Georg Baselitz (and others), this design hotel has reasonable rates, good in-house food and drink options and friendly staff. €

LUX 11 MAP PAGE 58, POCKET MAP F12. Rosa-Luxemburg-Str. 9–13 ⓤ Rosa-Luxemburg-Platz ⓦ lux-eleven.com. This designer apartment-hotel oozes style and has big, comfy rooms (with kitchenettes and spacious, open bathrooms) and a decent restaurant–bar. **€**

NIKOLAI RESIDENCE HOTEL MAP PAGE 58, POCKET MAP E13. Am Nussbaum 5 Ⓤ Klosterstr. Ⓦ nikolai-residence. com. Cute and well-run 3-star hotel in the heart of the Nikolaivertel. Decor is fairly modern and dotted with paintings and photos by German artists, and the 21 rooms are simple, reasonably stylish and comfortable. **€€**

PARK INN MAP PAGE 58, POCKET MAP f12. Alexanderplatz 7 Ⓤ / Ⓢ Alexanderplatz Ⓦ parkinn-berlin.de. This towering 37-floor GDR-era building is more welcoming on the inside than the out. Unexciting but comfortable rooms feature cosy beds, marble bathrooms and, past the twentieth floor, panoramic views across Berlin. Gym, sauna and a rooftop terrace, too. **€€**

Potsdamer Platz and Tiergarten

BERLIN MARRIOTT HOTEL MAP PAGE 66, POCKET MAP A15. Inge-Beisheim-Platz 1 Ⓦ berlinmarriott.de. This business hotel is a surprisingly dynamic spot for leisure travellers too. Located right on Potsdamer Platz, it boasts a slick bar, an excellent restaurant (*Midtown Grill*), plus a pool and comprehensive fitness centre. **€€**

HOTEL HANSABLICK MAP PAGE 66, POCKET MAP B5. Flotowstr. 6 Ⓤ Tiergarten Ⓦ hansablick.de. The *Hansablick*, located right on the water, has rooms with balconies and/or river views and a traditional interior that features artworks by the likes of Otmar Alt and Heinrich Zille. Rates include breakfast, wi-fi and parking. **€**

RITZ CARLTON MAP PAGE 66, POCKET MAP A15. Potsdamer Platz 3 Ⓢ/Ⓤ Potsdamer Platz Ⓦ ritzcarlton.com. This distinctive skyscraper hotel has 303 rooms with expensive cherry-wood closets and watercolour paintings. There are also bars, a tea lounge, a great brasserie, and fantastic five-star service. Breakfast included. **Doubles from €€€€**

SHERATON BERLIN GRAND HOTEL ESPLANADE MAP PAGE 66, POCKET MAP D6. Lützowufer 15 Ⓤ Nollendorfplatz Ⓦ esplanadeberlin.com. Smack between Ku'damm and Potsdamer Platz, this large, smart hotel has two restaurants, a New York-style cocktail bar and a spa. **€€**

Prenzlauer Berg

EASTSEVEN MAP PAGE 78, POCKET MAP F10. Schwedter Str. 7 Ⓤ Senefelderplatz Ⓦ eastseven.de. Laid-back hostel located on the border of Mitte and Prenzlauer Berg. Rooms (singles, doubles, twins, dorms) and public areas are clean and functional, furnishings are decent quality and there's a lounge area with books and board games. No stag or hen groups. **€**

HOTEL TRANSIT LOFT MAP PAGE 78, POCKET MAP K3. Immanuelkirchstr. 14a Ⓤ/Ⓢ Alexanderplatz Ⓦ transit-loft.de. A modern hotel set in a nineteenth-century, yellow-brick factory and well located for Kollwitzplatz (see page 77). The 47 rooms (dorms included) are airy and well lit with basic furnishings and en-suite showers. **€**

LETTE'M SLEEP MAP PAGE 78, POCKET MAP J3. Lettestr. 7 Ⓢ Prenzlauer Allee Ⓣ 030 44 73 36 23. Located directly on Helmholtzplatz, this vaguely hip backpacker hostel has basic but clean dorms (four- to seven-bed) as well as twins and private apartments. There's a common room, kitchen (but no breakfast), free wi-fi and a beer garden in summer. **€**

MYER'S HOTEL MAP PAGE 78, POCKET MAP J3. Metzer Str. 26 Ⓤ Senefelderplatz Ⓦ myershotel.de. Set in a nineteenth-century Neoclassical building, this tasteful hotel has 51 rooms in a range of shapes and sizes, a glass-roofed courtyard with lounge and gallery with changing exhibitions. There's also a garden with terrace. **€€€**

PFEFFERBETT MAP PAGE 78,

POCKET MAP F10. Christinenstr. 18–19 ⓤ Senefelderplatz ⓦ pfefferbett.de. This welcoming hostel has clean, smart rooms and dorms, a buzzy lobby and a lovely courtyard garden that doubles as a beer garden. Bicycle hire, guided tours and laundry services available. €

Friedrichshain

A&O BERLIN FRIEDRICHSHAIN MAP PAGE 78, POCKET MAP B17 Boxhagener Str. 73 ⓢ Ostkreuz ⓦ aohostels.com. A good hostel choice if you're travelling with kids, with family rooms alongside the usual selection, plus a children's games room and a large garden – childcare is even offered at weekends. €

LOCKE AT EAST SIDE GALLERY MAP PAGE 92, POCKET MAP L6. Mühlenstr. 61–63 ⓢ Ostbahnhof ⓦ lockeliving.com/en/berlin. Design-led aparthotel situated right next to the East Side Gallery overlooking the River Spree, featuring 176 spacious and contemporary apartments, some with balconies and river views. You can stay here for as little as one night or up to a few months. There's also a gym, co-working space, Mediterranean restaurant and chic cocktail bar with DJs throughout the week. €€

MICHELBERGER MAP PAGE 92, POCKET MAP M7. Warschauer Str. 39–40 ⓤ Warschauer Str. ⓦ michelbergerhotel.com. Creative, welcoming and trendy, the rooms here are imaginatively and individually designed, the stylish lounge area has regular gigs and the drinks and food are good. €€

NHOW MAP PAGE 92, POCKET MAP M7. Stralauer Allee 3 ⓢ Warschauer Str. ⓦ nhow-berlin.com. This four-star concept hotel merges a music theme with designer hotel rooms. Recreational amenities include a health club, sauna and fitness facility and some rooms have great views over the river. €

VIENNA HOUSE BY WYNDHAM ANDEL'S BERLIN MAP PAGE 92, POCKET MAP M3. Landsberger Allee 106 ⓢ Landsberger Allee ⓦ wyndhamhotels.com. This sprawling design hotel has 557 small and retro-ish rooms with full amenities and spacious bathrooms. The top-floor *Skykitchen* and *Skybar* have great city views and there's a 550-square-metre spa. €€

West Kreuzberg

CINDERELLA.KREUZBERG MAP PAGE 102, POCKET MAP G8. Mehringdamm 57 ⓤ Mehringdamm ⓣ 030 86 00 80 33. Lovely, quiet boutique hotel in a former chocolate factory. The hotel is set back from the road and surrounds a lovely courtyard making it a particularly peaceful place to stay. The rooms are cosy and include thoughtful touches that make you feel at home. €

GRAND HOSTEL MAP PAGE 102, POCKET MAP F7. Tempelhofer Ufer 14 ⓤ Möckernbrück ⓦ grandhostel-berlin.de. Set inside a listed historic building near the Landwehr Canal, this award-winning hostel ups the ante in terms of elegance and space. There's a bar and library room on site, furnishings are design-savvy and the bright, stylish rooms and dorms don't have bunks. €

JOHANN HOTEL MAP PAGE 102, POCKET MAP H8. Johanniterstr. 8 ⓤ Prinzenstr. ⓦ hotel-johann-berlin.de. Close to Bergmannstrasse and the Jewish Museum, the *Johann* is a fairly nondescript but friendly hotel, with spacious rooms and a peaceful garden. €

MÖVENPICK HOTEL MAP PAGE 102, POCKET MAP F7. Schöneberger Str. 3 ⓢ Anhalter Bahnhof ⓦ movenpick.accor.com. This former Siemens office has a unique mix of contemporary and industrial decor: Philippe Starck pieces in the rooms, wood and glass in abundance and a pleasant courtyard restaurant and bar. €

East Kreuzberg

COMEBACKPACKERS MAP PAGE 108, POCKET MAP J7. Adalbertstr. 97 ⓤ Kottbusser Tor ⓦ comebackpackers.com. This friendly hostel has big, bright bedrooms and a large cosy common room overlooking Kottbusster Tor. There's a 24-hour bar, foosball, a book exchange and plenty of board games to keep you entertained. €

MOTEL ONE BERLIN-MITTE MAP PAGE 108, POCKET MAP J7. Prinzenstr. 40 ⓤ Moritzplatz ☎ 030 69 56 71 740, ⓦ motel-one.com. Well located for Alexanderplatz and the Oranienstrasse scene, this functional hotel has comfortable enough rooms with all necessary conveniences, a bar for snacks and drinks and free wi-fi. €

Charlottenburg

25HOURS HOTEL BIKINI BERLIN MAP PAGE 122, POCKET MAP B6. Budapester Str. 40 ⓤ /ⓢ Zoologischer Garten ⓦ 25hours-hotels.com. The hotel that single-handedly funked up West Berlin, the 25hours comes with a playfully cool design aesthetic, quirky bedrooms and a fabulous rooftop restaurant and bar (see page 131). The Kaiser Wilhelm Church is right across the street. €€

AM STEINPLATZ MAP PAGE 122, POCKET MAP B6. Steinplatz 4 ⓢ Zoologischer Garten ☎ 030 55 44 440, ⓦ marriott. com. Sumptuous boutique set inside a heritage-listed building that was once the haunt of the more well-heeled and intellectual Weimar set. Rooms are richly appointed with a mix of vintage and modern furnishings and there's a top-notch restaurant and classy bar with craft beer and occasional DJs. €€

ART HOTEL CHARLOTTENBURGER HOF MAP PAGE 122, POCKET MAP A6. Stuttgarter Platz 14 ⓢ Charlottenburg ⓦ charlottenburger-hof.de. Bright contemporary hotel, replete with modern art, Bauhaus design and multicoloured furniture. Perks include an on-site café-restaurant with terrace and courtyard. Rates can often be slashed by booking specials online. €

HOTEL Q! MAP PAGE 122, POCKET MAP A6. Knesebeckstr. 67 ⓤ Uhlandstr. ⓦ hotel-q.com. One of west Berlin's swankiest hotels, the Q! has bathtubs built into bed frames, elegantly minimal rooms, chocolate massages and the Fox! Bar, plus a lounge and garden. €€

HOTEL ZOO MAP PAGE 122, POCKET MAP B6. Kurfürstendamm 25 ⓤ Kurfürstendamm ⓦ hotelzoo.de. This historic hotel's 144 rooms are sumptuously appointed with tasteful fashion photographs and high-quality wooden floors and furnishings. There's a restaurant and lounge, and two sixth-floor penthouse suites if you feel like splashing out. €€

SANA HOTEL MAP PAGE 122, POCKET MAP B7. Nürnberger Str. 33–34 ⓤ Augsburger Str ⓦ berlin.sanahotels.com. A short stroll from the KaDeWe and Berlin Zoo (see page 120), this well-designed hotel has 208 rooms (of which 13 are suites and 42 apartments), a restaurant and a chill-out bar/lounge, indoor pool, sauna and fitness facilities. €€

Schöneberg

ARTHOTEL CONNECTION MAP PAGE 132, POCKET MAP C7. Fuggerstr. 33 ⓤ Wittenbergplatz ⓦ arthotel-connection. de. Hetero-friendly gay hotel located near KaDeWe in the gay village. Most rooms are large and en suite, bright, pleasant and ordinary; the "playroom", however, comes with chains and slings. €

JUGENDHOTEL BERLINCITY MAP PAGE 132, POCKET MAP E9. Crellestr. 22 ⓤ Kleistpark ⓦ jugendhotel-berlin. de. With 170 plain but comfy beds in a renovated factory building, this is a good option for budget-conscious travellers. Pool tables, decent rooms and a convivial bar. €

ESSENTIALS

Beach bar on the River Spree

Arrival

By air

Flying is, predictably, the cheapest and most convenient way to get to Germany from overseas, as well as from many other European countries thanks to the proliferation of discount airlines.

Berlin Brandenburg Airport (BER) is now the sole international airport serving the city. Located in Schönefeld, 18 km south-east of the centre of Berlin, the airport opened in 2020.

The modern airport (ⓦ ber. berlin-airport.de) is in Berlin public transport's zone C. An ABC ticket that will take you into the city centre costs €4.40 and can be purchased from any of the machines at the airport's railway station and from bus drivers. Tickets must be validated before use, using the yellow or red boxes on the train platform or inside buses.

The railway station, **Flughafen BER**, can be found in Terminal 1 on level U2. The airport express service, FEX, connects the airport with the city centre, reaching Berlin's central train station, the Hauptbahnhof, in around 30 minutes. The FEX leaves the airport twice an hour, while regional trains RE8, RB22, RB23, RB24 and RB32 run frequently between the airport and the centre. S-Bahn lines S9 and S45 run regularly (every 10–20min) to main stations like Alexanderplatz (38min), the Hauptbahnhof (44min) and Bahnhof Zoo (50min).

Local bus stops can be found on the arrivals level of Terminal 1. Express bus services #X7 (N7 at night) and #X71 run every 20min to nearby U-Bahn Rudow. The journey takes approx. 14mins. BER2, an express service between Potsdam and the airport, runs several times a day.

Taxis can be found outside Terminal 1 on level E0. Expect to pay €50–80 to get to the city centre.

By train

Germany is well connected by train with destinations throughout continental Europe. Check Deutsche Bahn's excellent website (ⓦ bahn. de) for international routes. From the UK, a slow but comfortable option is via Paris, with the overnight sleeper departing three times a week from

City tours

Original Berlin Walks ⓦ berlinwalks.de. Offers a range of walking tours of between three and six hours, many of which cover the main sights and beyond. Prices vary according to tour.

Trabi Safaris ⓦ trabi-safari.de. Drive around the city (slowly) in a Trabant, the car of choice for the GDR (with guides and without) with live information delivered to you via radio. Day and night "safaris" available.

Slow Travel Berlin ⓦ slowtravelberlin.com. English-speaking cultural/historical walking tours (2hr), mostly run by long-term residents.

Alternative Berlin ⓦ alternativeberlin.com. Street art tours, pub crawls and other "alternative culture" trawls.

Berlin Music Tours ⓦ musictours-berlin.com. Follow the musical trails of Bowie, Iggy Pop, Depeche Mode and U2.

Paris Est (total travel time from London around 16hr); a quicker daytime route is via Brussels and Cologne (from 10hr 30min).

The huge **Hauptbahnhof** northeast of the Brandenburg Gate is well connected to the rest of the city by S- and U-Bahn. Many long-distance routes also stop at Ostbahnhof, convenient for Friedrichshain, or Bahnhof Zoo, for Charlottenburg. All are well connected by S-Bahn.

By bus
Several private bus companies, such as Flixbus (ⓦflixbus.com), run routes from as far afield as Barcelona and Bucharest.

Most international buses stop at the bus station (ZOB), linked to the centre by express buses #X34 and #X49, as well as regular buses #104, #139, #218, #349 and #M49; U-Bahn #2, from Kaiserdamm station; and S-Bahn from Messe-Nord/ICC.

Getting around

U- and S-Bahn
BVG (ⓦbvg.de) operate an efficient, integrated system of U- and S-Bahn train lines, buses and trams. During the week, U-Bahn trains run 4am–1am, while S-Bahn trains run from 4.30am–1.30am. Both run all night on Fri & Sat.

Buses and trams
The city bus network – and the tram system mainly in eastern Berlin – covers most of the gaps left by the U-Bahn; several useful **tram** routes centre on Hackescher Markt, including the M1 to Prenzlauer Berg.

A night-time network of buses and trams operates, with buses (around every 30min) often following U-Bahn line routes; free maps are available at most stations.

Buses #100 and **#200** drive past many famous Berlin sights en route from Zoologischer Garten to Alexanderplatz, providing a cheap alternative to a sightseeing tour.

Tickets and passes
Tickets are available from machines at U-Bahn stations, on trams or from bus drivers. Zone AB **single tickets** cost €3.50; zone ABC single €4.40; **short-trip tickets** (Kurzstreckentarif) are available for three train or six bus/tram stops for €2.40; zone AB **day-tickets** cost €9.90.

Validate single tickets in the yellow machines on platforms or aboard buses/trams before travelling.

For two–six days the **WelcomeCard** (see page 154) is good value.

Bike rental and tours
Cycling in Berlin is easy, safe and very popular. Not only is the city (mostly) as flat as a pancake, there are dedicated cycle lanes throughout.

There are also numerous rental places, including: Fat Tire (ⓦfattirebiketours.com/berlin), beneath the TV tower at Alexanderplatz. They also offer half-day **bike tours.** Nearly all hostels rent bikes for around €14/day. Share bikes can be found at stations across the city, both traditional bikes and e-bikes; reservations are primarily app-based.

Taxis
Taxi fares are €4.30 flag-fall plus €2.80/km for the first 3km, then €2.60/km up to 7km and €2.10 thereafter; if you hail a taxi on the street – rather than at a stand or by phone – you can ask for a short-trip price (Kurzstreckentarif) before the trip starts and pay €6 for a 2km ride. Taxi firms include: Taxi Funk (☏030 44 33 22 ⓦtaxifunk-berlin.de) and Funk Taxi (☏030 26 10 26 ⓦfunk-taxi-berlin.de).

Directory A–Z

Accessible travel

Most U-Bahn stations and ninety percent of S-Bahn stations in Berlin and the surrounding area are accessible. Buses and trams marked with a wheelchair symbol are equipped for passengers with disabilities, and a footnote on the printed schedule provided at every stop indicates which trams and buses are so equipped. Look for the words *behindert* (disabled) and *ausgestattet* (outfitted). Both buses and trams also have seat-belt-like straps to prevent a wheelchair from rolling during transit.

Addresses

If you are looking for an address in the former East, bear in mind house numbers run in different directions on each side of the street, as opposed to the usual odd/even system.

Children

Berlin is a surprisingly child-friendly city. There are public playgrounds all over the city (many created from transforming bombed-out areas), plenty of green areas to play in such as Tiergarten, Volkspark Friedrichshain and Viktoriapark, and, in the colder months, kindercafés (see *Kiezkind*, page 86) where parents can enjoy a frothy coffee while their kids enjoy the toys.

Cinema

Movies in English play at Babylon Berlin (ⓦ babylonberlin.eu), Babylon Kreuzberg (ⓦ yorck.de), Kino International (ⓦ yorck.de) and more.

Crime and emergencies

Serious crime is relatively low in Berlin, though petty crime such as bike theft can be rife. You can get help at any police station where English is usually spoken. Reporting thefts at local police stations is straightforward, but inevitably there'll be a great deal of bureaucracy to wade through. **Emergency numbers** are: police ☏ 110; fire and ambulance ☏ 112.

Discount passes

The **WelcomeCard** (Berlin AB: 48hr €26, 72hr €36, 5-day €49; Berlin and Potsdam ABC: 48hr €31, 72hr €41, 5-day €53; ⓦ berlin-welcomecard.de) includes public transport and up to fifty percent off at many of the major tourist sights. Though the standard card doesn't cover Museum Island, a version that does include these museums is available. Many of the discounts are the same as student prices.

Electricity

230 V, 50 Hz. The Continental two-round-pin plug is standard.

Embassies and consulates

Australia, Wallstr. 76–79 ☏ 030 88 00 880; Canada, Leipziger Platz 17 ☏ 030 20 31 20; Ireland, Jaegerstr. 51 ☏ 030 22 07 20; New Zealand, Friedrichstr. 60 ☏ 030 20 62 10; South Africa, Tiergartenstr.18 ☏ 030 22 07 30; UK, Wilhelmstr. 70–71 ☏ 030 20 45 70; US, Pariser Platz 2 (postal address Clayallee 170) ☏ 030 83 050.

Health

Emergency room at Campus Charité Mitte (entrance Luisenstr. 65/66), ☏ 030 450 531 000. Most doctors speak English. Pharmacies (Apotheken) can deal with minor complaints; all display local pharmacies open 24hr, including Apotheke Hauptbahnhof, at the Hauptbahnhof.

Internet

Free wi-fi at the The Center at Potsdamer Platz and at other public malls and spaces, and in most hotels and hostels. Internet cafés charge around €1.50/30min.

LGBTQIA+ Berlin

Berlin's diverse gay scene is spread across the city, but with a focus of sorts in Schöneberg, especially around Nollendorfplatz. The magazine *Siegessäule* (ⓦ siegessaeule.de) has listings and can be picked up in many cafés and shops. Club nights by GMF, including Sundays at *Ritter Butzke*, are always worth checking out. The Christopher Street Day Pride festival takes place every year in July (ⓦ csd-berlin.de).

Listings and websites

The Berliner is a monthly English-language magazine focusing on arts and music listings in Berlin (ⓦ the-berliner.com). The two main listings magazines in German are *Tip* (ⓦ tip-berlin.de) and *Zitty* (ⓦ zitty.de); all are widely available in cafés and bars. For adverts and classifications also check Craig's List Berlin (ⓦ berlin.craigslist.org). Useful English-language websites include ⓦ iheartberlin.de and ⓦ slowtravelberlin.com.

Lost property

Allegedly only 25 percent of lost items in Berlin turn up again, but it's worth contacting Zentrales Fundbüro, Platz der Luftbrücke 6 (ⓣ 030 75 60 31 01), who will help you with the search (there are six such offices around the city). Left or lost luggage can also be reclaimed at both airports and at the Lost & Found section at the Deutsche Bahn. Look for the "Fundbüro" at Rudolfstr. 1–8 if you lost something in the subway or tram, or contact BVG-Fundbüro (ⓣ 030 29 74 33 33 ⓦ bvg.de/en/service-and-support/lost-and-found).

Money and banks

The German currency is the euro (€). Exchange facilities are available in most banks, post offices and commercial exchange shops called **Wechselstuben**. The Reisebank has branches in most main train stations (generally open daily, often till 10/11pm) and ATMs are widespread. Basic **banking hours** are Monday to Friday 9am to noon and 1.30 to 3.30pm, Thursday till 6pm. **Credit cards** are fairly widely accepted – but certainly not universally; independent or smaller restaurants and cafés often don't take them. There can be a surcharge in hostels and smaller hotels.

   ATMs and exchange are at the airports, and major stations including: Reisebank, at the Hauptbahnhof (daily 8am–9pm), Zoo station (daily 8am–9pm), Friedrichstr. station (daily 8am–8pm) and Ostbahnhof (Mon–Fri 8am–9pm, Sat & Sun 8am–8pm).

Opening hours

Larger shops open at 8am and close around 6 to 8pm weekdays and 2 to 4pm Saturday, and often close all day Sunday; smaller shops often open

---

Eating price codes

Each restaurant and café reviewed in this Guide is accompanied by a price category, based on the cost of a **two-course meal (or similar) for one, including a non-alcoholic drink.**

€ = Under €16
€€ = €17-25
€€€ = €26-35
€€€€ = over €35

at 11am/noon and keep quite erratic hours. Pharmacies, petrol stations and shops in and around train stations stay open late and at weekends. Museums and historic monuments are, with a few exceptions, closed on Monday.

Phones

Call shops are the cheapest way to phone abroad, though you can also phone abroad from all payphones except those marked "National"; phonecards are widely available. The operator is on ☎ 03.

Post offices

Post offices are open Monday to Friday 8am to 6pm and Saturday 8am to 1pm. There's a convenient branch at Lehrter Str. 1, near Berlin's main train station, Hauptbahnhof.

Smoking

After a wave of restrictions on smoking in all bars was introduced, a lawsuit from a small bar owner resulted in the law being loosened, and Berlin bars are pretty much almost all back to being smoky or having smoking areas. Expect to get smoke in your eyes in almost all bars that don't serve food. All restaurants are smoke free, but many offer a smokers' lounge somewhere.

Sports and outdoor activities

Bundesliga football (ⓦ bundesliga. de) is the major spectator sport in Germany, with world-class clubs playing in top-notch stadiums, many revamped for the 2006 World Cup such as the Olympic stadium. Important matches sell out well in advance; tickets can be purchased from the clubs' websites.

Time

Berlin is on Central European Time (CET), one hour ahead of Britain and six hours ahead of EST, with the clocks going forward in spring and back again in autumn on the same dates as the rest of the EU, although whether this will continue in the future is currently in question. Generally speaking, Berliners, like the rest of Germany, use the 24-hour clock.

Toilets

There are a few public toilets (*Öffentliche Toilette*, WC) some of which you'll find in the almost romantic-looking toilet huts in parks and close to the subway. In some, you have to put a €0.50 coin in the slot to open the door. There are mostly free toilets at petrol stations, where you have to ask the clerk for the key. Also big shopping centres have public toilets normally with a maintenance woman, who you should tip around €0.30–50. Gentlemen should head for *Herren*; ladies should head for *Damen*.

Tipping

If you're in a group, you'll be asked if you want to pay individually (*getrennt*) or all together (*zusammen*). In general, round your bill up to the next €0.50 or €1 and give the total directly to the waiter when you pay (rather than leaving it on the table afterwards).

Tourist offices

The main contact details are: ☎ 030 25 00 25 33, ⓦ visitberlin.de. Tourist offices at: Hauptbahnhof (daily 8am–9pm) and Brandenburg Gate (daily 10am–6pm).

Festivals and events

Berlinale

February ⓦ berlinale.de

For two weeks each year, Berlin turns into Hollywood as the Berlinale international film festival takes over the town. Around four hundred films are shown every year as part of the Berlinale's public programme, the vast majority of which are world or European premieres.

Impro

March ⓦ improfestival.de
Running since 2001, this event is the biggest improvisation theatre festival in Europe. Its goal is to show international developments and take part in an intercultural exchange with different ensembles.

Gallery Weekend

End April/early May ⓦ gallery-weekend-berlin.de
Fifty-plus galleries and small venues dedicated to design and art open for one weekend to present exclusive exhibitions and contemporary international art.

My Fest

May 1 ⓦ myfest36.de
Kreuzberg open-air festival, with music and cultural events and a lot of food stalls (especially around Kottbusser Tor). Note that May Day demonstrations in the evening in the same area have a tendency to turn ugly, though the daytime is usually very safe and fun.

Carnival of Cultures

May ⓦ karneval.berlin
This colourful weekend street festival has been running since 1996, with four music stages featuring acts from around the world, plus culinary delights and handmade arts and craft stands. The peak of the festivity is a street parade with around 4800 participants from eighty nations on Whitsunday.

Fête de la Musique

June ⓦ fetedelamusique.de

Over ninety concerts are put on all over town to celebrate the Fête de la Musique, a hugely ambitious event that happens across 520 cities.

Christopher Street Day (CSD)

June/July ⓦ csd-berlin.de
Held in memory of the first big gay uprising against police assaults in Greenwich Village (the Stonewall riots), Berlin's biggest Pride celebration has been running since 1970 and draws around half a million people.

Classic Open Air

July ⓦ classicopenair.de
Five days of classical music at the beautiful Gendarmenmarkt. Previous events have included London's Royal Philharmonic Orchestra performing the complete James Bond title themes and The Scorpions performing with the German Film Orchestra Potsdam.

Long Night of the Museums (Lange Nacht der Museen)

August ⓦ lange-nacht-der-museen.de
As summer draws to a close, the Long Night of the Museums is when many of Berlin's museums stay open late into the night – usually until midnight or much later – with special programmes and events.

International Literature Festival

September ⓦ literaturfestival.com
Berlin's biggest literary event celebrates "diversity in the age of globalization" and features an eclectic and international selection of writers over twelve days.

Berlin Art Week

Mid-September ⓦ berlinartweek.de
Started in 2012, Berlin Art Week offers an exciting and richly varied programme of outstanding exhibitions, openings and events at ten participating institutions.

Berlin Marathon

Late September ⓦbmw-berlin-marathon.com
First held in 1974, Berlin's marathon traditionally takes place on the last weekend in September. With around forty thousand participants from around one hundred countries, it's one of the largest and most popular road races in the world.

Festival of Lights

Mid-October ⓦfestival-of-lights.de
Every autumn, Berlin's famous sights are transformed into a sea of colour and light, including the Brandenburg Gate, the Berlin TV Tower, Berliner Dom and more. The nightly light show comes with art and cultural events around the topic of light.

Berlin Jazz Festival

Early November ⓦberlinerfestspiele.de
Running since 1964, the Berlin Jazz Festival is a world-renowned event that presents all the diverse styles of jazz. The full and varied programme is traditional and progressive in equal parts, and has tended to focus in particular on big bands and large ensembles.

International Short Film Festival

Mid-November ⓦinterfilm.de
The five-day International Short Film Festival Berlin was founded in 1982 and is today Berlin's second-largest international film festival. The event showcases numerous competitions across all genres, as well as workshops and parties.

Christmas Markets

December
Many public locations in Berlin, such as Gendarmenmarkt, Alexanderplatz and the Schloss Charlottenburg, are taken over by Christmas markets selling arts, crafts, Glühwein, Wurst, pancakes and more.

Chronology

720 The region known today as Berlin is settled by Slavic and Germanic tribes.

948 Germans take control over the area of present-day Berlin.

983 The Slavs rebel (successfully) against German rule.

Twelfth century Germans take over the land again.

1244 Berlin is first mentioned in written records.

1247 The city of Cölln is founded right next to Berlin.

1307 Cölln and Berlin become known simply as "Berlin", the larger of the two cities.

1451 Berlin becomes the royal residence of the Brandenburg electors and has to give up its status of a free Hanseatic city.

1539 The city becomes officially Lutheran.

1576 Nearly five thousand inhabitants of Berlin are wiped out by the bubonic plague.

1618 The devastating Thirty Years' War begins. Half of Berlin's population left dead.

1685 Friedrich Wilhelm offers asylum to the Huguenots. More than fifteen thousand come to stay in Brandenburg and six thousand eventually settle in Berlin.

1699 Inauguration of Schloss Charlottenburg, commissioned by Sophie Charlotte, wife of Friedrich I.

1701 Berlin becomes the capital of Prussia.

1740 Friedrich II – known as Frederick the Great – comes to power and rules until 1786. He turns Berlin into a centre of Enlightenment.

1745–47 Sanssouci Palace is built as the summer palace of Frederick the Great.

1788–91 The Brandenburg Gate is built by Carl Gotthard Langhans.

1806 Napoleon conquers Berlin but grants self-government to the city.

1810 Humboldt University is founded by Prussian educational reformer and linguist Wilhelm von Humboldt.

1841 The Museum Island is dedicated to "art and science" by Friedrich Wilhelm IV of Prussia.

1861 Wedding, Moabit and several other suburbs are incorporated into Berlin.

1871 Berlin becomes the capital of a unified German Empire, under Otto von Bismarck's chancellorship.

1894 The Reichstag opens.

1918 Berlin witnesses the end of World War I and the proclamation of the Weimar Republic.

1920 Berlin established as a separate administrative zone with the Greater Berlin Act. A dozen villages and estates are incorporated into the city.

1923 Tempelhof is officially designated an airport.

1933 Adolf Hitler comes to power.

1939 The beginning of World War II.

1938–45 Thousands of Jews (and other minorities) living in Berlin are sent to death camps.

1943–45 Seventy percent of Berlin is destroyed in air raids.

1945 The Allies take Berlin, and divide it into four zones.

June 1948 The Berlin airlift sees Allied planes delivering supplies to West Berlin.

1949 The Federal Republic of Germany is founded in West Berlin and German Democratic Republic in East Berlin.

June 1953 An uprising of industrial workers against the Communist regime is brutally put down.

August 1961 The building of the Berlin Wall begins.

June 1963 US President John F. Kennedy visits West Berlin, delivering his famous speech, "*Ich bin ein Berliner*".

1972 Access is guaranteed across East Germany to West Berlin with the Four Powers Agreement.

1987 During his second Berlin visit, Ronald Reagan makes a speech in front of the Brandenburg Gate, demanding Mr Gorbachev "tear down this wall!"

1989 Following mass demonstrations across East Berlin, the border crossings are finally opened on November 9.

October 3, 1990 The two parts of Berlin are unified as part of the Federal Republic of Germany.

1997 Peter Eisenman's controversial design for a Memorial to the Murdered Jews of Europe is chosen.

1999 Berlin becomes capital of a reunified Germany and the German government and parliament begin their work in Berlin.

2005 Openly gay mayor Klaus Wowereit dubs Berlin "poor but sexy", which becomes a slogan for the city.

2006 The new Hauptbahnhof is opened.

2008 Tempelhof airport is officially closed; the surrounding area is later turned into a public park.

2009 Twenty years since the fall of the Wall is celebrated with a "Festival of Freedom". Visiting dignitaries include Mikhail Gorbachev and Bill Clinton.

2014 Structural work on new Stadtschloss (City Palace) completed; opens as the Humboldt Forum in 2020.

2014 Germany beat Argentina 1–0 in the World Cup Final.

2015–16 Berlin takes in a million refugees.

2016 12 people die during a Christmas market terror attack in Berlin.

2017 High speed railway is opened between Berlin–Munich reducing travel time from 6hrs to 3hrs 45min.

2018 Over 200,000 people march and protest against the rise of far-right populism in Berlin.

2019 On 9 November, Berlin celebrates 30 years since the fall of the Berlin Wall.

2020 Berlin Brandenburg Airport opens.

2024 Berlin's Olympiastadion hosts the final of Euro 2024. Spain beat England 2–1.

German

Being the cosmopolitan city it is, it's fairly easy to get around Berlin using English. That said, it's worth learning some basics in case you find yourself needing to communicate in the native language. Needless to say, any attempt at speaking German often goes a long way.

Alphabet
Umlaut: ä, ö, ü are the letters that have the mysterious Umlaut in the German language, which can also be spelled as ae, oe or ue. The ä is pronounced like the English a, the others are comparable to speaking the German o or u with a ping-pong ball in the mouth.
The "sharp S": Whenever the s is supposed to be emphasized in German,

the "sharp s", **ß**, is used, which is pronounced like the English double s. Since the spelling reform in 1996 there have been some discussions about whether to retain ß or use ss, but for now both variations are accepted.

Pronunciation
Consonants: "w" is pronounced like the English "v"; "sch" is pronounced "sh"; "z" is "ts". The German letter "ß" is basically a double "s".
Vowels: "ei" is "eye"; "ie" is "ee"; "eu" is "oy".

Basic words and phrases
Yes Ja
No Nein
Please Bitte
Thank you Danke

Good morning Guten Morgen
Good evening Guten Abend
Hello/Good day Güten Tag
Goodbye Tschüss, ciao, or auf Wiedersehen
Excuse me Entschuldigen Sie, bitte
Today Heute
Yesterday Gestern
Tomorrow Morgen
Day Tag
Week Woche
Month Monat
Year Jahr
Weekend Wochenende
Monday Montag
Tuesday Dienstag
Wednesday Mittwoch
Thursday Donnerstag
Friday Freitag
Saturday Samstag/ Sonnabend
Sunday Sonntag
I don't understand Ich verstehe nicht
How much is...? Wieviel kostet...?
Do you speak English? Sprechen Sie Englisch?
I don't speak German Ich spreche kein Deutsch
I'd like a beer Ich hätte gern ein Bier
Where is? Wo ist?
entrance/exit der Eingang/der Ausgang
Toilet das WC/die Toilette
Women Damen
Men Herren
Hotel das Hotel
HI hostel die Jugendherberge
Main train station der Hauptbahnhof
Bus der Bus
Plane das Flugzeug
Train der Zug
Cheap billig
Expensive teuer
Open offen/auf
Closed geschlossen/zu
Entrance Eingang
Exit Ausgang
Smoking/no smoking rauchen/nicht rauchen
1 Eins
2 Zwei
3 Drei
4 Vier
5 Fünf
6 Sechs
7 Sieben
8 Acht
9 Neun
10 Zehn
11 Elf
12 Zwölf
13 Dreizehn
14 Vierzehn
15 Fünfzehn
16 Sechszehn
17 Siebzehn
18 Achtzehn
19 Neunzehn
20 Zwanzig
21 Ein-und-zwanzig
22 Zwei-und-zwanzig
30 Dreissig
40 Vierzig
50 Fünfzig
60 Sechzig
70 Siebzig
80 Achtzig
90 Neunzig
100 Hundert
1000 Tausend

Food and drink

Terms and phrases

Breakfast Frühstück
Lunch Mittagessen
Coffee and cakes Kaffee und Kuchen
Dinner Abendessen
Knife Messer
Fork Gabel
Spoon Löffel
Plate Teller
Cup Tasse
Glass Glas
Menu Speisekarte
Starter Vorspeise
Main course Hauptgericht
Dessert Nachspeise
The bill Die Rechnung
Organic Bio
Vegetarian Vegetarisch

Basics

Brot bread
Brötchen bread roll

GERMAN

Butter butter
Ei egg
Essig vinegar
Honig honey
Joghurt yoghurt
Käse cheese
Kuchen cake
Marmelade jam
Milch milk
Öl oil
Pfeffer pepper
Reis rice
Sahne cream
Salz salt
Scharf spicy
Senf mustard
Sosse sauce
Suppe soup
Zucker sugar

Drinks

Bier beer
Eiswürfel ice cube
Flasche bottle
Kaffee coffee
Leitungswasser tap water
Mineralwasser mineral water
Saft juice
Sprudelwasser sparkling mineral water
Stroh straw
Tee tea
Teekanne teapot
Wein wine
Weissbier/Weizenbier wheat beer

Meat (Fleisch) and fish (Fisch)

Currywurst sausage served with a curry powder and tomato ketchup
Forelle trout
Garnelen prawns
Huhn, Hähnchen chicken
Kabeljau cod
Lachs salmon
Lamm lamb
Lammkotelett lamb chop
Leber liver
Leberkäse meatloaf
Makrele mackerel
Rindfleisch beef
Schinken ham

Schweinefleisch pork
Speck bacon
Thunfisch tuna
Wiener Schnitzel breadcrumb- coated cutlet, usually veal but sometimes pork
Wurst sausage
Zander pikeperch

Vegetables (Gemüse)

Blumenkohl cauliflower
Bohnen beans
Bratkartoffeln fried potatoes
Erbsen peas
Grüne Bohnen green beans
Gurke cucumber or gherkin
Karotten, Möhren carrots
Kartoffel potatoes
Knoblauch garlic
Lauch (or Porree) leeks
Maiskolben corn on the cob
Paprika peppers
Pilze or Champignons mushrooms
Pommes frites chips or fries
Rosenkohl Brussels sprouts
Rotkohl red cabbage
Salat salad
Salzkartoffeln boiled potatoes
Sauerkraut pickled cabbage
Spargel asparagus (white asparagus is particularly popular in season)
Tomaten tomatoes
Zwiebeln onions

Fruit (Obst)

Apfel apple
Banane banana
Birne pear
Erdbeer strawberry
Himbeer raspberry
Kirsch cherry
Orange orange
Zitrone lemon

Desserts and cakes

Eis ice cream
Käsekuchen cheesecake
Keks biscuits
Kuchen cake
Schokolade chocolate
Torte cake/tart

Publishing Information

Sixth edition 2024

Distribution

UK, Ireland and Europe
Apa Publications (UK) Ltd; sales@roughguides.com
United States and Canada
Ingram Publisher Services; ips@ingramcontent.com
Australia and New Zealand
Booktopia; retailer@booktopia.com.au
Worldwide
Apa Publications (UK) Ltd; sales@roughguides.com

Special Sales, Content Licensing and CoPublishing

Rough Guides can be purchased in bulk quantities at discounted prices. We can create special editions, personalised jackets and corporate imprints tailored to your needs. sales@roughguides.com.

roughguides.com

Printed in Czech Republic

This book was produced using **Typefi** automated publishing software.

A catalogue record for this book is available from the British Library

The publishers and authors have done their best to ensure the accuracy and currency of all the information in **Pocket Rough Guide Berlin**, however, they can accept no responsibility for any loss, injury, or inconvenience sustained by any traveller as a result of information or advice contained in the guide.

Rough Guide Credits

Editor: Beth Williams
Cartography: Carte
Picture editor: Piotr Kala
Picture Manager: Tom Smyth
Layout: Ankur Guha

Original design: Richard Czapnik
Head of DTP and Pre-Press: Rebeka Davies
Head of Publishing: Sarah Clark

About the Author

Matthew Pearson is a writer and ghostwriter based in London, ex of Berlin. He enjoys going everywhere on foot and eating well on the cheap.

Acknowledgements

Thanks to Beth, Jean, Amanda, Nic and Isi.

Reader's updates

Thanks to all the readers who have taken the time to write in with comments and suggestions (and apologies if we've inadvertently omitted or misspelt anyone's name): Jonathan Bardill, Josephine Bryan, Gabriele Chi, Paul Collinson, Caroline Dale, Pierre Flener, Jack Howell, Helen Knox, Gareth Logue, Gloria Sebulsky

Help us update

We've gone to a lot of effort to ensure that this edition of the **Pocket Rough Guide Berlin** is accurate and up-to-date. However, things change – places get "discovered", opening hours are notoriously fickle, restaurants and rooms raise prices or lower standards. If you feel we've got it wrong or left something out, we'd like to know, and if you can remember the address, the price, the hours, the phone number, so much the better.

Please send your comments with the subject line "**Pocket Rough Guide Berlin Update**" to mail@uk.roughguides.com. We'll credit all contributions and send a copy of the next edition (or any other Rough Guide if you prefer) for the very best emails.

Photo Credits

(Key: T-top; C-centre; B-bottom; L-left; R-right)

AMANO Bar 37
Big Brobot 98
Burg & Schild 61
Café Einstein Stammhaus 54
Clärchens Ballhaus 22T
Diana Jarvis/Rough Guides 12T, 18MC, 93, 141
Grüne Baumpython/Aquarium Berlin 121
Helmut Meyer zur Capellen 142/143
iStock 2BC, 5, 11B, 12/13B, 14T, 16T, 24/25, 40, 41, 43, 56, 60, 80, 94, 125, 137
Mundo Azul 82
Oliver Mahne/Oliv 63

Roger d'Olivere Mapp/Rough Guides 10, 12B, 14B, 15B, 15T, 18TC, 18MC, 19TC, 20TC, 20MC, 21TC, 21MC, 21MC, 22B, 23MC, 34, 42, 65, 71, 73, 77, 86, 100, 101, 104, /105, 110, 113, 115, 126, 129, 131, 134
Shutterstock 1, 2TL, 2BL, 2MC, 4, 6, 11T, 12/13T, 16B, 17T, 17B, 19MC, 19MC, 20MC, 22MC, 23TC, 23MC, 27, 30, 31, 33, 35, 36, 38, 44. 45, 47, 50, 52, 53, 57, 59, 62, 67, 68, 69, 70, 72, 74. 75, 87, 88, 89, 90, 91, 95, 96, 97, 99, 103, 106, 114, 118, 119, 124, 127, 128, 130, 133, 135, 138, 140, 150/151
Zula 85

Cover: Tram at Alexanderplatz **Shutterstock**

Index